# RELIGION AND
# EDUCATION

# RELIGION AND EDUCATION

*Edited by*
*Willard L. Sperry*

BY

ALEXANDER MEIKLEJOHN
PAYSON SMITH
HOWARD MUMFORD JONES
VICTOR L. BUTTERFIELD
THEODORE FERRIS

*66921*

*Essay Index Reprint Series*

LIBRARY

## BOOKS FOR LIBRARIES PRESS
### FREEPORT, NEW YORK

Originally published as Volume IV of
Religion in the Post-War World

Copyright 1945 by the
President and Fellows of Harvard College

Reprinted 1971 by arrangement with
Harvard University Press

INTERNATIONAL STANDARD BOOK NUMBER:
0-8369-2202-6


LIBRARY OF CONGRESS CATALOG CARD NUMBER:
76-142698


PRINTED IN THE UNITED STATES OF AMERICA

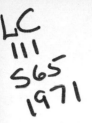

LC
111
S65
1971

✗ Sten Gros. 2

## CONTENTS

# INTRODUCTION

CHRISTIANITY and Judaism, because they are "book religions," are usually identified as learned religions. This means that they have each a body of doctrine to be passed on from generation to generation. They are therefore committed to an educational process and faced by an educational problem.

Whether religion ever can be "taught" is perhaps an open question. The ideas which it presupposes and the faith which it formally professes can be told to each oncoming generation, but whether these ideas will eventually come alive as a personal and intimate conviction remains to be seen. St. Augustine was probably nearer the mark when he said that "one loving heart kindles another." Plainly the best pedagogic methods need to be supplemented by the force of example and the contagion of appealing personality. Since religion is a type of experience which is as closely identified with the arts as with the natural sciences it cannot be taught as geology is taught. Information must be supplemented by all that is meant by personal taste, and that intimate identification of the self with a subject which we call appreciation.

On the other hand every learned religion must make a

sincere and sustained effort to perpetuate its body of pro-
fessed truth. Failure to do so would be suicidal. Whatever
he may make of the faith of his fathers in his maturity,
every child and youth is entitled a knowledge of the religion which he inherits as part of the culture to which he belongs. Religion has played a great part in making America
what it is today. Any attempt to delete religion from the
record of the past and any attempt to describe contemporary American life as a whole in purely secular terms will be
false to the facts. Youth which comes of age in ignorance of
the facts is deprived of part of its intellectual birthright and
is to that extent uneducated.

The problem is complicated in America by the separation
of church and state. Tax-supported institutions are in general prohibited from anything but the most casual religious
practices, and the most oblique references to religion in
the class room. The bulk of the teaching done in America
has to be done in the public schools and the state universities. The case with privately supported institutions is different; yet even there a studied secularity is the academic
fashion with many, if not most, faculty members.

Meanwhile, we have mounting evidence in our American
schools and colleges of a steadily increasing religious illiteracy. This illiteracy bodes ill for the character of the
country in days to come. When youth is denied both the
spiritual ideals and the moral restraints of religion, it has
lost one of the influences which have made America what it
has been thus far.

To the difficult and delicate problems which arise in this

field the following contributors to this volume have addressed themselves with candor and good courage.

Alexander Meiklejohn, after holding academic posts at Brown University, Amherst College, and the University of Wisconsin, has been, until most latterly, Chairman of the School for Social Studies in San Francisco. He is at present in Government service in Washington.

Payson Smith, for many years the honored and efficient Commissioner of Education in the Commonwealth of Massachusetts, is at present Acting Dean of the School of Education at the University of Maine in Orono.

Howard Mumford Jones, author, critic, and man of letters-at-large, after serving at the Universities of Texas, North Carolina, and Michigan, has been for ten years Professor of English in Harvard.

Victor L. Butterfield, one of the most active members of the National Council on Religion in Higher Education, is President of Wesleyan University in Connecticut.

Theodore P. Ferris, rector of Trinity Church in Boston, familiar and welcome guest preacher at Harvard, occupies one of the most historic and influential pulpits in America.

Willard L. Sperry
*Editor*

*Harvard University*
*Cambridge, Massachusetts*

*Religion
and
Education*

#### ✦ 1 ✦

# From Church to State

THREE hundred years ago Anglo-American teaching was done chiefly by the church. In early days English and American education was, in the main, created and sustained, inspired and controlled, by religious groups. But, today, in the greater part of the Protestant world, at least, education is secular. The school has been, or is being, cut off from the church. With the exception of some "private" schools and colleges it has been taken over by another social institution. What institution is that? As matter of sober fact, who is now in charge of the teaching of our people?

There can be no doubt that, with conscious intention or without it, Anglo-American Protestant civilization has drifted into an answer to that question. It is the state which is replacing the church. It is government, national, provincial, or local, which has control of teaching. Education is not only becoming secular. It is also becoming political. It is not simply Russia, Germany, and Italy which have made the state the successful rival of the church. In spite of all our protestations to the contrary, we have been busy for

3

three hundred years effecting the same revolution. We have, in fact, led the way. At the most crucial point in the field of social action we have ousted religion and put government in its place. Our protestations do not mean that we deny the fact. They mean only that, as good Anglo-Saxons, we are reluctant to face it. But the time has come when we must face it. The crucial, the decisive problem of our culture is that of the nature and functions, the powers and limitations, of the political state. That is what England and Germany are fighting about. That is the issue with which America is most deeply concerned. We must see, therefore, how, in the field of teaching, the conflict between democracy and despotism, between reason and violence, has forced itself upon us.

From church to state! In three centuries we Protestants have transferred from one of these institutions to the other the task of shaping the minds and characters of our youth. Do we realize what we have done? This is revolution. It is the most fundamental aspect of the social transformation which has brought us from the medieval into the modern world. As compared with it, changes in the gaining and holding of property, the making and enforcing of laws, even the expression of experience in literature and art, are secondary and superficial. In the transition from the medieval to the modern form of human living I doubt if any other change is as significant as the substitution of *political* teaching for *religious*. We have changed our procedure for determining what kind of beings human beings shall be.

The significance of the change from church to state can

be measured only if one can measure the difference between the purposes of these two institutions. Traditionally we have regarded them as differing widely in sphere and function. One of them we have called spiritual, the other, prudential. They have, in fact, often been intensely hostile to one another. Churches have tried to lead men in one direction. Governments have been the agents of different motives. And, this being true, it seems to follow that, during the last three hundred years, the intention of education must have radically changed. Has it? What were schools for when the churches controlled them? What are they for now, as our governments support and direct and use them? And, further, can we infer from the fact that political institutions are replacing those of religion, that the two have more in common than we have usually believed? No institution can teach unless it is equipped with the ideas, the appreciations, the wisdom out of which alone teaching can be made. If, at this point, the state is to take the place of the church, then it may be that the state is, or will become, much more like the church than we have commonly thought it to be. What, then, are the human motives to which religious and political teaching have given expression?

The explanation of the fact that it was the church which first created and maintained the school seems fairly clear. In an earlier Europe it was generally recognized that the churches were the guardians of our "way of life." They had convictions about the nature of the world and of man. And from this it followed that they knew how men should live. The churches could define and prescribe the goodness of living and, in large measure, its truth and beauty as well. Speaking with the voice—or the voices—of God, they held authority to mark out the values and customs of our behavior. They were able to teach men and women and children how to live because they knew, as did no other institution, what life should be. They had beliefs and values which could be used for the concrete guidance and control of human behavior. That was their social function. And it was out of those beliefs and values that their control of education came.

If, then, political governments are taking the place of the churches in the making and directing of education it follows that we must ask what are the beliefs and values which those governments express and represent. The city of New York, or San Francisco, or Middletown, has schools whose task it is to prepare young people for living. What do those cities believe about living? What lessons have they to teach? Does New York City believe anything? Has it any values or convictions out of which a scheme of teaching may be made?

Here is, I am sure, the most terrifying question with which present-day education is faced. There may have been a time when the common tastes and beliefs of our American communities were so active, forceful, and articulate that they could take cultural dominance over the lives of their individual members, young and old. But times have changed. We are no longer certain what a nation or state or county or town or village believes, if indeed it believes anything. And with that doubt comes the fear that our teaching is likewise lacking in conviction. Culturally a school system cannot rise higher than its source. If a government means little to its citizens then the teaching which is given by its schools will mean just as little to its pupils. We face, therefore, a most urgent question with regard to the public schools and colleges of our contemporary civilization. Are our governments, national, provincial, and local, culturally fitted to do the work which we have assigned them? Have they the wisdom of mind, the strength of character, the sensitiveness of appreciation, which are needed by anyone who is to take charge of the development of the thinking and the attitudes of a people? Can the state replace the church, as we Anglo-Saxons have summoned it to do?

As we prepare to deal with this question two explanatory remarks should be made. First, when we speak of the transferring of the school from the church to the state we are describing, not what should have happened, but what has happened. We are not saying, as yet, that the change is good. Nor are we condemning it as bad. We are simply recording a fact. Whether anyone intended it or not, the change has taken place. With some few striking exceptions education in the United States is today politically controlled. And there is no likelihood that it will become private or religious again. We Americans cry out, especially against Russia and Germany, because they have made teaching political, have declared and provided that the churches shall have no part in the training of youth. And yet, in our own different but equally effective Anglo-Saxon way, we have been taking the same action. We do not talk about it as do the Russians and Germans. As already noted, we are unwilling to admit it even to ourselves. And yet we have done it. Educationally, we are revolutionists. We must face the plain and inescapable fact that in our future, so far as we can see, the teaching of our people will be done chiefly by our governments.

And, second, it is a curious feature of this revolutionary transfer of power from church to state that, for the most part, it has happened with the consent, and even on the initiative, of the churches themselves. Slowly, it is true, especially in England, and reluctantly in many cases, these churches have deprived themselves of one of their most cherished prerogatives. We Protestants have torn our teaching loose from its roots. We have broken its connection with the religious beliefs out of which it had grown. The typical Protestant has continued to accept the Bible as, in some sense, the guide of his own living but, in effect, he has wished to exclude the Bible from the teaching of his children. The teacher in the modern school is commissioned to teach many things. But he is not commissioned—he is rather forbidden—to teach that "faith" upon which the community, for which he teaches, has built its own character and intelligence.

We have said that our Protestant-capitalist civilization is involved in a dilemma. As we enter upon the attempt to discover the ideas and motives out of which that dilemma arises it may be worth while to note some of the forms which our fears and doubts are taking. They give striking evidence of the inner contradictoriness, the mental distractedness, of the culture to which we belong.

First, it seems to many of us quite possible that our educational revolution has been a colossal blunder. How do we know that governments can teach? The churches, it is true, had not done too well with the task. But they were, at least, in purpose and spirit, suited to the teaching enterprise. They were concerned with beliefs and values. But on what evidence have we based the opinion that the state can take charge of the cultivation of intelligence? Is the state primarily an agency of understanding? Is it the human *mind* in action? It may be that, without clear realization of what we were doing, we have been driven by the pressure of events into ways of teaching which are doomed to failure. There are many critics of current education who would approve that suggestion. They would tell us that the learning which is being created under government direction is pseudo learning, that the teaching which is given by a state is pseudo teaching. They would remind us that the unfitness of the church for a task does not prove the fitness of the state to do it. Are they right? Is education by government inherently false in principle, futile in practice? If so, our predicament is a desperate one. Under present circumstances to say that public education is, of necessity, a failure would seem to be the most unequivocal way of saying that our American culture is doomed. For better or for worse, we have chosen to put the guiding and nurturing and cultivating of the growth of our people into the hands of the state. And we must go through with the experiment. If it succeeds, we succeed. If it fails, we fail. It is, so far as I can see, "our" way of dealing with the problem of the making of a human society and a human education. And we must take its consequences.

If, however, the venture of government education is to have a fair trial, two traditional Anglo-Saxon attitudes toward the state must be seriously questioned. We Protestant-capitalist democrats, in our zest for individual freedom, have been accustomed to think of political controls as hostile to that freedom. As individuals we have feared the encroachments of government upon our rights, our liberties, our independence. That dread in its most extreme form is expressed by the words of H. M. Tomlinson as he defines a human attitude in *All Our Yesterdays:*

"My church is down," I hear him saying. "My God has been deposed again. There is another god now, the State, the State Almighty. I tell you that god will be worse than Moloch. You had better keep that in mind. It has no vision; it has only expediency. It has no morality, only power. And it will have no arts, for it will punish the free spirit with death. It will allow no freedom, only uniformity. Its altar will be a ballot-box, and that will be a lie. Right before us is its pillar of fire. It has a heart of gun metal and its belly is full of wheels. You will have to face the brute, you will have to face it. It is nothing but your worst, nothing but the worst of us, lifted up. The children are being fed to it." [1]

[1] H. M. Tomlinson, *All Our Yesterdays* (New York: Harper & Brothers, 1930), p. 436.

Such words as these reveal our fundamental incoherence and self-contradiction. The state, we say, has no vision, no arts, no morality, no freedom. It is our worst. It is a brute. Its name is Moloch. Therefore, we make it the teacher of our children. Could there be any more convincing evidence of the distractedness of a culture? Is there any wonder that, in planning for our own lives and those of our children, we are obsessed by anxiety and horror and confusion of mind?

A second attitude less extreme in its antagonism toward the state is that of regarding it as merely negative, as merely an agency of regulation and of limitation rather than of active creation.[2] It is one of the curious contradictions of the Protestant era that for three centuries we have both enlarged the powers of government and tried to diminish them. We have been going in two different directions at once. On the one hand, as in the case of education, our corporate interests have inevitably and enormously extended political activities. But, on the other hand, our prevailing political mood has been that of interpreting the state as merely setting limits within which the active behavior of

[2] R. M. MacIver in his book *Community* (New York: Macmillan, 1920) says, "Because it can determine only the external forms of conduct, the law of the State must be mainly (though by no means wholly) negative. It must for the most part be content (as the neo-Hegelians themselves are forced to admit, though they do not see the force of the admission) to 'hinder hindrances' to social welfare. It can prevent or punish wrong-doing rather than endorse right-doing" (p. 35). That assertion that the action of government is mainly "negative," our argument will be attacking throughout its course. To regard as merely "hindering hindrances" the institution which is now, for the most part, in charge of learning and of teaching is to cut the roots of social intelligence, both intellectual and practical.

individuals and groups must be kept. In this mood, we think of government as a necessary evil, called into being, not by any positive values of its own, but only by the unavoidable clashes of those creative agencies by which the real work of the world is done. It has even been said, on high authority, that that is the best government which governs least. But if we are to have state education, such an attitude is no longer possible. Its absurdity becomes unendurable. An institution which teaches a society is not negative. An agency which provides for the advancement of learning, which makes, out of learning, an education for all the people—that institution is not simply preventing something from being done. It is doing something. It is creating a society. It is fashioning human beings. It is directing the course of a civilization. It is—as the church was—a constructive enterprise.

Here then, in its educational form, is the crucial problem of our contemporary culture. It is the source of the dilemmas underlying the Great War. What is the relation between government and intelligence? We Anglo-Saxons, when we put the activities of teaching into the hands of the church, were saying, whether we knew it or not, that the church was the agency of understanding. Wisdom, we thought, came from God. And the churches, as the representatives of God among men, could therefore take charge of the creating and imparting of that wisdom by which the activities of men are made kind and reasonable. The church could teach.

But it is equally clear that this responsibility has now

been, or is now being, transferred by us to the institutions of government. And that can only mean, if we know what we are doing, that the state is now, for us, an institution, the primary institution, of intelligence. Human government is human understanding in action. To know, then, what a state is we must know what intelligence is. And vice versa, to know what intelligence is, we must understand what political agencies are and do. What, then, is the state? Does it speak for reason? Or is it primarily an agency of force, of violence? Any genuine study of education must make its way into and, one hopes, through, the complications of that network of problems. It is a long road to travel but, so far as I can see, it is the only road which leads, under contemporary conditions, to human peace and freedom.

II

If we assume, then, that the assertions, and even the hopes, of theology are gone, that their claim to validity is now negligible, the basic problem of our "modern" society is thrust upon us. Our civilization, our culture in all its variations, our ways of life, all these have been propped up by theological belief. In law, in medicine, in art, in literature, in politics, in science, in morals, in social theory, in education, men have assumed the existence and validity of cosmic principles on the basis of which their work could be, and would be, judged. Though men have striven for human ends, they have done so as servants of God. And now that presupposition is being abandoned. We know no "cosmic" principles of intelligence. We know no "divine" standards or ends.

And that fundamental change in belief confronts us with the desperate issue which, at every significant point in our experience, staggers the modern mind. If we can no longer believe in God can we maintain, can we carry on, the civilization which was founded on that belief? Is not civilization itself a veneer, a pretense? The despair which underlies that query has been cutting deep into the foundations of all our institutions. And it still remains to be seen whether that despair can be dispelled, whether confidence can be put in its place, whether, within its own experience, mankind can find a solid basis on which to continue, to enlarge, to enrich its culture. It is that question which we must answer if we are to have a theory of modern education.

The loss of religious faith is, as many of us know, a shattering experience. Individuals have felt in their own lives its bitterness, its disillusionment. And the last three centuries of Protestantism in Europe and America give all too obvious evidence of its destructive, disintegrating consequences for the social order. If one has really believed that the principles of freedom, of justice, of generosity, of sensitiveness, of intelligence, are established by God, the loss of the belief that there is a God seems, at first sight, to smash the whole structure of human insight and aspiration.

And, yet, even in the midst of the agony and confusion of the first shock of that experience, one can find evidence that all is not lost. There is, I am sure, a human basis for a new building, for a reconstruction of the old building. Civilization can go on.

In the first place, it requires courage and honesty and

love of truth to enable a man to discard a belief upon which his whole pattern of life, as well as that of his community, has been established. To say "I will not believe beyond the warrant of the evidence which bears upon the question at issue" is to have a principle to whose authority one submits one's thinking. And that principle evidently holds good whether God exists or not. It is by the authority of that principle that one questions the existence of God. It may be, then, that underlying all our standards of conduct and opinion we can find, in human nature itself, a warrant quite as adequate, more adequate than that which the belief in God had given. There may be human "reasons" for truth and freedom, justice and generosity, which can well replace the divine "reasons" which have previously been given.

And, second, if God does not exist, if the assertions about him are myths, then the very presence of those myths is a fact of supreme importance for our knowledge of mankind. The Bible, for example, depicts the spiritual life of man as seeking conformity to principles which God has "required of us." But if God does not exist, who formulated those principles? Who wrote the Bible? It seems clear that God did not do so. Nor did he even "inspire" men to do it. But that implies that the insights, the aspirations of the Bible were created by men, created by their own unaided efforts. The truth is, then, that human prophets have perceived in human nature itself the beauty of holiness, the strength of humility, the magnificence of wisdom. And these qualities seemed to them so great, so significant in their authority

over the beliefs and the conduct of men that without knowing what they were doing, they created the myth of divine
origins and divine sanctions. That myth is now fading
away. But the human truth to which it gave untenable expression still remains. Courage, beauty, truth, freedom, justice, honesty are still the original facts. The myth was a
secondary thing. Its going need not affect the primary values which it was intended to serve. As the sanctions of religion fail us, one consolation is still available. If human values had not been, in and of themselves, good, no sanction
by a God could have made them so. Among all the beings
whom our imagination might have created no one of them
would have been regarded by us as divine unless he had had
"reasons" for what he did, what he approved. And when he
goes, the "reasons" remain. Our modern task is to find
them, to interpret them, to use them, in their new setting.

But the myth which we discard leaves behind it more
than consolation. It gives also guidance for study. In the
form of religious belief men have thrown upon a cosmic
screen their most profound convictions, their deepest insights about themselves. And this means that in the linea-
ments of the God whom he has imagined, man can discover
his own features. If we can know what that God, in the
words of theology, has "required of us" then we can know,
in modern words, what we require of ourselves. If we can
discover why, in our story about him, he made those requirements, then we can be sure why we should make them,
why we have made them. It will be necessary, as our argument advances, to note the fact that the theological form of

statement has distorted and falsified the picture of human nature and human destiny. One cannot use myths as if they were facts without suffering serious consequences of error and illusion. And yet, as the myth is put aside, we can find beneath it the truth from which the myth drew its meaning, its power. What, then, as we look back upon the religious beliefs of our Protestant faith, are the basic ideas and values upon which the structure of our civilization rests? And, especially, what part does intelligence play in that human enterprise which men have described to themselves in mythical terms?

In answer to this question I venture two assertions. First, the basic belief of our culture—a belief which our religion has both maintained and concealed—is that men are brothers. Human beings have kinship with one another. And, second, all those activities which we sum up under the term "intelligence" are expressions of that kinship, rest upon it as a final fact. In the meaning of those two statements is to be found, I believe, all that we have available for the making of a general theory of education.

When we say that men are brothers we are saying that, both morally and intellectually, they are engaged in a common enterprise. That enterprise determines what are, and what should be, their relations to one another. It prescribes both their modes of conduct and their modes of thought. When we have said, in the past, that God created men in his own image, that he cared for them, and that they, therefore, should care for one another, what we were really saying was that human insight has disclosed life to be such that it cannot be lived rightly or intelligently unless men deal with one another as if they were brothers. We were, in that imaginative picture, laying down the fundamental principles of an organized society. Those principles were, of course, only vaguely and inaccurately seen. By differing creeds and sects they were conceived in multitudes of varying ways. And yet, running through all these aberrations we can find a constant clue to guide us in our study. The dogma of the fatherhood of God, which we ourselves created, which, for many centuries, we have maintained, to which, in words at least, we still appeal when basic issues are at stake—that dogma tells us that the men and women of our culture have found the fundamental moral and intellectual fact of human living to be the brotherhood of man. It suggests that, for human aspiration and purpose and intelligence, if not yet for human achievement, mankind is a fellowship.

### III

The peculiar significance of Rousseau for our Western culture lies in the fact that he leads the way in the substitution of the state for the church as the primary institution of human brotherhood. The belief in fellowship which had formerly been expressed in religious terms he now expresses in terms of politics. As the church loses its grip on the essential principles of human society and human education, Rousseau so describes the state as to qualify it for taking the empty place. The state is, for him, the agency of fellowship. It is, therefore, the source of all morality. And, for the same reason, it is the source of intelligence. Political institutions, as he sees them, are the deliberate attempt of human beings to live together in that friendship which only mutual understanding can give.

If Rousseau is right, we can answer with a strong affirmative the question with which our argument started—can a state teach? Schools and colleges can be, and should be, conducted by governments. But is he right? To minds steeped in Anglo-American competitive individualism, he seems not only wrong but also absurd. And yet I am sure that he is right. If we wish to see clearly those principles of morality and intelligence upon which all theories of education must rest, there is, I am sure, no better line of approach than that which appears if one follows with careful and sympathetic study the attempt of Rousseau to understand that human institution which we call "the state."

There are two conflicting types of political theory. On the one hand is the "organic" theory which Rousseau represents. Opposing it are "disorganic" theories, such as those of Locke and Dewey. Organic theories explain social action in terms of a striving for order and coherence. This does not mean that they find San Francisco or Peru or Cook County to be a well-organized and unitary enterprise. It means only that, in the midst of a vast multiplicity of interests and influences, these human groups have the task of creating unity of idea and purpose. In so far as they are reasonable that is what they accomplish. Disorganic theories, on the other hand, explain societies in terms of multiplicity. They find them to be external collocations of indi-

viduals and groups. Each of these has its own purpose or
purposes. But the collocation, as a whole, has no purpose.
The relations within it are mechanical rather than organic.
They are relations of power or of force. This is the
"pressure-group" theory of society. Its abstractions ignore
the morality and the intelligence which Rousseau sees as the
primary characteristics of a political society.

Rousseau's analysis of the state as an agency of general
intelligence is very incomplete. He was not a technical logician. He speaks much more easily about a general will
than about a general mind. He himself was keenly aware of
the inadequacy of his own work. The *Social Contract,* he
tells us, was only a partial answer to a wider problem about
which he had been puzzling for some twenty-two years before 1762. That answer left much to be done, much which
has not yet been done. And still, he does go to the heart of
the problem. He has an amazing capacity for defining an
issue, for sensing an opposition. Rousseau tells us that, in so
far as a state is constituted, its individual members give over
to it all that they are, all that they have, whether of rights or
of possessions, and that the state uses these for the good of all.
In this formula he faces squarely the paradox which has tor-
mented political theory throughout the course of modern
Protestant-capitalism. How shall we combine the freedom of
the individual with the authority, the organic unity, of the
state? How shall we say that each citizen "owns by right" the
property of all?

"The problem is," Rousseau tells us, in words already

quoted, "to find a form of association which will defend
and protect with the whole common force the person and
goods of each associate and in which each, while uniting
himself with all, may still obey himself alone, and remain as
free as before." The "whole common force" is to be in the
hands of the state. But each individual is to be free. He is to
"obey himself alone." To the problem of making that seemingly impossible combination, "the Social Contract finds a
solution." It reads as follows: "Each of us puts his person
and all his possessions in common under the supreme direction of the general will, and, in our corporate capacity, we
receive each member as an indivisible[3] part of the whole." [4]
It is those two statements, giving the political problem and
its political answer, which establish Rousseau as the first of
the "moderns." He succeeds, or at least he points the way
toward success, in formulating in secular terms the political
relationship which, in the medieval era, had been defined by
religion and theology. And the striking fact is that the
meaning which that theology tried to express remains un-
changed. The "Christian" tradition is maintained. The
structure of civilization which that tradition had supported,
still stands. "Whosoever will lose his life for my sake shall
find it" was the old doctrine. It is now replaced by the assertion that each of us, in a well-organized society, yields to
the state all that he is, all that he has, and that, in doing so,

[3] This word should be, I think, "inseparable."
[4] Rousseau, *The Social Contract* (New York-London, Everyman's
Library, [1913]), p. 15.

each of us becomes a free person. We give ourselves and our possessions "without reserve." And thereby we find our own persons, our own rights and goods, protected by the full force of the community. And, further, as we share in the common will, the common devotion to the common welfare, each of us finds himself "obeying himself alone, and thus as free as he was before.[5]

Is that a valid account of the political relationship? The best way to test it is to confront it with such an explicit, conscious attitude as is taken by our people whenever the Constitution of the United States is accepted as the supreme law of the land. The Preamble to the Constitution reads, "We, the people of the United States, in order to form a more perfect union, establish justice, insure domestic tranquillity, provide for the common defense, promote the general welfare, and secure the blessings of liberty to ourselves and our posterity, do ordain and establish this Constitution for the United States of America." Does Rousseau express the meaning, the intention of that action? It seems to me that he does. By the adoption of the Constitution, every man who becomes a citizen of our government, agrees that he himself, his family, his possessions, his rights, shall be placed within the legal jurisdiction, under the political authority, of the nation. And, further, he expects that, through that common agreement—and only through such an agreement—he and his fellows will win practical security and spiritual freedom. They will become free members of a self-governing society.

[5] Rousseau should have said "free as he was not before."

IV

Today it is commonly said that the exaltation of the state is hostile to the dignity and freedom of the individual. That statement seems to me both logically false and practically disastrous. The will of a democratic state is as little antagonistic to the dignity and freedom of the human individual as has been, in the religious field, the Will of God. As against that fallacious, though popular, doctrine, my argument may be summed up in a single assertion. If that assertion is true, the argument stands. If it is false, the argument falls.

The assertion to which I refer is this—all the activities which give a man dignity are done "for the state." And, vice versa, the test of any government is found in the dignity and freedom, the equality and independence, of its citizens. It exists through and for them, just as they exist through and for it.

The principle just formulated can be understood only if we make a distinction which the political theorizing of our Protestant-capitalist culture has perversely obscured. Every citizen of a democratic state has two different relations to his government. In a government which is carried on by the consent of the governed every citizen is both governor and governed. He is both ruler and ruled. As ruler, he shares in the making and administering of political decisions. As ruled, he is subject to the decisions which are made. But these two roles of the individual are radically different in kind. And the error of the individualistic theory of society is that it confuses them. It demands for men as governed rights which belong to them only as governors. It denies to men as rulers, a dignity which can be denied them only in so far as they are subjects. If we can clear away that confusion, our social principle will be ready for application in the field of education.

Now, if this distinction is made it becomes clear that men have dignity only in so far as they are rulers, only in so far as they share in the attempt to advance the common welfare. And, further, only as rulers have men a right to liberty. When a man is using his mind and will in dealing with matters of public policy, that mind and will must be kept free. The public welfare requires it. That is what is intended by the magnificent first sentence of the Bill of Rights in which the government itself declares that not even the government shall limit the liberty of religion or speech or press or assembly or petition. When, on the other hand, a man is pursuing his own private interests, when, therefore, he is one of the governed, there is no reason why his activity should be free from regulation. On the contrary, it is of the very essence of government that "private" activities should be regulated and controlled as the public interest may require. That distinction between the citizen, as ruler, who is promoting the general welfare and the same citizen, as ruled, since he is carrying on his own business, is essential to any clear understanding of what we mean by "liberties" and "rights" in a democratic society.

Now the point which I am making is that if we wish to understand human dignity, freedom, and independence we must see men acting as rulers of the state. That state rests upon a social agreement that life shall be made reasonable. But such reasonableness can be created only by individuals who act for the state, rather than for themselves. It is that spiritual achievement which gives men dignity, which reveals their freedom and independence. What Englishmen did achieve greatness, as individuals, during the Industrial Revolution? Was it those who piled up possessions for themselves or who held fast to wealth and power handed down to them by their ancestors? If one thinks that, let him read again the words in which Matthew Arnold describes the "Barbarians" of the upper classes. These men, he tells us, were, in their idealessness, "forever asleep." But the men and women who have been magnificent through all the ghastly horrors of the transition from an agricultural to an industrial economy were persons who "lost themselves" in public causes. Bright and Cobden, Carlyle and Mill, Florence Nightingale and John Henry Newman—these were thinking, not of themselves but of England and, in their higher moments, of a human society wider than England. And, in our own day, side by side with the courage and audacity of a Churchill, one may place the brilliant studies of John Maynard Keynes or the scholarly and magnanimous insights of Richard Henry Tawney. These men and women have dignity because they are thinking and acting "for the state," identifying themselves with it. They plan for the war and for the peace of their people. They analyze the financial and industrial and social influences of their people. They grapple with the intellectual and moral problems of their people. They are rulers. They are disinterested. In so far as that is true, the state is not their enemy. It is themselves.

### V

As we seek the consummation of our argument, logical coherence as well as spiritual insight would require of us that we advance beyond Rousseau to Rousseau's greater pupil, Immanuel Kant. In the Metaphysic of Morals, the Principles of Political Right, the Eternal Peace, Kant lays down the only workable basis for the moral organization of human society and, hence, for the teaching of the future.

These two prophets of the world to come are telling us that the human road through the ages leads from violence to reason, from barbarism to civilization. So far as they are intelligent, men seek to establish reasonable relations with their fellows. Such relations are not possible with mosquitoes or tornadoes or trees. But they are possible with normal human beings. And the human task, so far as men are moral and intellectual, is that of extending the scope of reasonable coöperation to its widest and deepest limits. The final goal of that attempt would be the creation of a world-state, in which the appeal to reason would have replaced the resort to violence in the relations of all men to one another.

If we accept for humanity the goal which our argument has suggested, the ruling motive of education becomes clear. Learning is not merely the acquiring of mastery over intellectual subject matter. It is, first of all, initiation into many social groups and, ultimately, into one social group. The teacher leads his pupil into active membership in a fraternity to which he himself belongs. The motive force of that fraternity is found in a common devotion to a common, coöperative enterprise. Just as, in the home, each child learns, or should learn, to play his part in the family circle, so, in our schools and colleges, every citizen of the world should become "at home" in the human "state." He should acquire a sense of what humanity is trying to do, and a will to join in doing it.

The calling of the teacher, as so defined, is one of infinite difficulty. But it is also infinitely significant. He is commissioned to form and fashion both human society as a whole and the individuals of whom that society consists. He acts for the state with a completeness of responsibility which is equaled by no other official.

If we accept the belief that the whole world of human behavior can be dealt with as a single enterprise which a single coöperative human intelligence is trying to direct, and if we regard all lesser enterprises as finding their basic justification and criticism as participants in this all-inclusive attempt, some general conclusions concerning education seem to follow.

First, governments, local, provincial, national, and supernatural, are equipped to teach. The handing over of the control of education from the church to the state has not been a fatal blunder. The state is not Moloch. It is not "nothing but your worst, nothing but the worst of us, lifted up." On the contrary, the state is the best of us, trying to control and to elevate the worst of us. It is ourselves seeking to be reasonable, to live in justice and freedom with one another. Man, at his best, is a political animal. His wisdom creates manners and morals. The same wisdom, when institutionalized, creates laws, roads, hospitals, parks, pensions, peace, schools. But these two expressions of wisdom are not hostile to one another. They are one in purpose, one in idea and value. And since that is true, education by the government is radically sound in principle. As our culture now stands, no other institution can equal the state as the representative of those purposes and beliefs which are the fruits of human reasonableness. We do not understand what a state is unless we see that it is both a student and a teacher. We belie its essential nature when we regard it as a policeman.

But, second, which of our governments shall take charge of education? Shall it be the village or the town or the country or the state or the nation or the world-nation? Each of these "states" represents a level of reasonableness. Each of them has its own "pattern of culture." And the choice among them is the choice of the subject matter of our teaching. Shall we teach young people to live in a village or in a nation or in the world? The answer to that question must not be oversimplified. Every human being needs to learn how to live in all the social groupings to which he "belongs." And yet, if our argument is valid, one principle emerges from it which is of primary importance. Fundamentally education belongs to the world-state. The reasonableness of that institution includes and criticizes all the lesser reasonablenesses of our experience. Every human being young or old should be taught, first of all, to be a citizen of the world, a member of the human fellowship. All other lessons are derivatives of that primary lesson.

From what has just been said it seems to me to follow that the control of education, its planning and basic administration should be in the hands of the world-state. It is, I think, obvious as we plan for the future, that the nation which is to include all the nations and rule over them must have military force sufficient to give it mastery over its members. It must have a legislature and an executive. It must have courts of justice. It must have an equitable and stable system of finance and trade. But more pressing than any of these is the need for a universal scheme of instruction, whose driving force shall be the purpose that all men shall live together in peace and freedom, with reasonable regard for one another. First of all, the world-state like any other state must be a teacher. If it cannot teach, it will do nothing else successfully.

If we are to have a world-state and to teach its lessons it is clear that the most difficult, as well as the most essential, education must be given, not to children but to men and women. As the new world takes form, the minds of children of every race and country will accept it as easily, more easily, than the chaotic, confusing, self-contradictory scheme of behavior which we now present to them. But that is not true of the grownups. We elders are caught in fear, in habit, in custom, in prejudice, in prudence, in common sense. It is we, therefore, who resist the education or reëducation which we need. If we are to have the moral and intellectual reconstruction which are implied in the making of a world-state, the prime essential is an adequate process of adult education. Our minds will have to be refashioned. And we ourselves must do it. There is no one else to teach us. We, members of a common humanity, acting together as one sovereign people, must teach ourselves to do and to be what our common citizenship offers us to do and be. We must learn so to know and care for all our fellow men that we can participate with them in the one common cause. That task of human self-education our generation is called upon to begin. But it will be only a beginning. The road to reasonableness goes on and on.

### VI

From church to state! From myth to fact! Can our culture make that transition? There can be little doubt, as Matthew Arnold has told us, that an old world is "dead." And for a long time now the new world has seemed "powerless to be born." And the essential guilt of "the three great democracies," Britain, France, and the United States, as well as of lesser democracies, has been their holding back in the face of the vast and terrifying possibility of a new birth. All over the world the new expression of the human spirit has been striving to break loose, to enter upon its career. Even the hysterical madness of the Germans and Italians and Japanese springs from the conviction that, the present chaos being intolerable, something better can be devised to take its place. The words of Adolf Hitler are madness. And yet that madness, as a power which threatens the peace and freedom of the modern world, does not spring primarily from the mind of Hitler. It is the madness of a civilization which has denied its own faith, which has been untrue to its own principles. If we believe in democracy we must practice it between nations as well as within our own nation. If we believe in freedom we cannot be content that other peoples shall be enslaved. If we believe in law and order we must join in establishing them for all mankind. If we believe in equality we cannot defend so desperately our own "higher standard of living." If we believe in reasonableness we must follow wherever reason may lead.

In the midst of all our agonies and uncertainties the new world is being born. It is that new world which gives meaning to education. Every pupil must be learning for it. Every teacher must be teaching for it. Every scholar must be thinking for it. Humanity is reasonable as well as unreasonable. It is the struggle between these two which defines the course of education. We know what teaching is only as we see and feel what the free spirit of man is trying to do and to be.

NOTE: This chapter is, in the main, the author's compilation of relevant passages from his recent book, *Education Between Two Worlds*, with certain editorial revisions and additions for use here. The editor and publisher of the present volume acknowledge with thanks permission to quote from the prior work, graciously granted by Harper and Brothers.

Payson Smith

*·2·*

# The Public Schools and Religious Education

For more than a century the people of the United States have shown a consistent determination to achieve two seemingly irreconcilable ends; one of them to keep sectarianism out of the public schools, and the other to keep religion in them.

Since sectarianism is something that can be fairly easily identified, and since laws and regulations about it can be framed with some clarity of meaning and intention, there has been considerable success in fulfilling the first of these purposes.

Since, on the other hand, there is an infinite variety of definitions of religion, it is not by any means easy to say how much religion there is, if any, in the public schools. There are those who maintain that there is none at all, while others insist that the public schools, in the substance of their offerings, the ends they aim for, and the methods they use, are potently religious.

32

This issue of the place of religion in public education has been in constant controversy throughout the entire period of the establishment and development of public education in this country.

Down to the very start of the constitutional era, education in the colonies, both public and private, had been to a great extent under the patronage and control of the church. This was especially the case in Massachusetts, whose early influence upon the other colonies and states was admittedly very great. In that colony, education was regarded as the handmaiden of religion; hence the church, the guardian of religion, was expected, as a matter of course and of right, to control and supervise the schools.

In the early records of the Massachusetts Colony there are numerous documentary witnesses to this close relationship of the government and the church in the conduct of education, and to the belief of the people that education under the church should be primarily devoted to religion and morals. Harvard College was established so that an educated ministry might be assured. It was against that "Old Deluder Satan" that the Great and General Court declared war when, in 1647, it ordered the towns to open common and grammar schools. In these schools reading was given first place so that the common man might have access to the Scriptures. Still further to insure the religious purposes of education, the clergymen of the towns were, by law, made the supervisors of the schools.

While the Puritan church was more closely identified with the government of Massachusetts than any church was with the government of any other colony, yet the views that were held in Massachusetts relative to education were, in some degree, present elsewhere. By the time of the Revolution, there had been a considerable modification of these views.

The controversies raging in western Europe about political and social theories, which were in part responsible for the Revolution here, were profoundly to affect education both in Europe and America. The effects were first practically felt here because, with the framing and adoption of the Constitution, the question of state-church relationship had to be settled. Following the decision in favor of the separation of church and state, it was then necessary to determine which one, the church or the state, was, in the new order, to control the schools. It was inevitable, in the prevailing circumstances, that the choice should fall to the state.

Before long, increased emphasis was placed upon civic and social objectives to the subordination of religious ones, and along with this increased emphasis upon secular aims of education there came changes in methods of teaching as well as in conceptions of discipline. The reforms that were advocated and adopted were bitterly opposed on the ground that they would destroy the influence of religion upon youth. The public schools, it was charged, would become irreligious and "godless." These charges were to be repeated many times by many people in succeeding years.

The recognition of the state as the responsible agency to support and control education was at first only implicit.

The federal constitution made no provision for it, reserving to the states complete discretion and authority over education. The people themselves had as yet by no means the clearer conceptions that later developed on the subject. Hence there was, of course, no sudden end of the former notion that education should primarily serve religion, nor indeed of the notion that the church ought to possess the schools.

Actually, church controls of education extended well into the first three or four decades of the last century. Nearly all secondary schools and colleges continued under denominational auspices. The post of the college presidency was still generally reserved to the clergy. During this period the common schools languished. This was no doubt owing to the gradual weakening of the long-established hold of the church over education and the as yet unawakened feeling of responsibility by the people for the support of a school system directed to civic and social goals.

For some time doubts and fears about secular aims of education were expressed chiefly by representatives of the Protestant churches, whose interest was no doubt stimulated by the church schisms which were taking place. All these earlier discussions went on in the absence of explicit provisions of constitution or statutes, so that, as can be imagined, policies were nebulous and practices were varied

II

About 1850, and rapidly thereafter, public opinion did crystallize through constitutional and statutory enactments.

Amendment after amendment has made it increasingly clear that the American people are committed in theory to the maintenance of public education supported by general taxation and open to all children on equal terms.

These amendments designed to protect the integrity of the public school system against any proposals to divide it were stimulated by the introduction of a new factor; namely the increasing influence of the Catholic Church and of one or two Protestant denominations which reopened, in a new form, the old issue of sectarianism.

These churches, holding that education and religion are inseparable, and that the church cannot avoid taking practically full responsibility for the education of its youth, hold that the generally accepted national policy involves injustice to them. They have taken the position that it is not fair to expect their communicants to contribute to the support of two systems of education, one through religious convictions, and the other through state policy. They contend that the civic and social objectives of church or parochial schools are not different from those of the public schools and that the state can achieve its own ends quite as well through the former as through the latter. So, it has been argued, the policies of the states should be so modified that public funds may be allocated to the support of parochial schools, at least for that part of their work which is secular in character. The views of these denominational groups have not been accepted. Indeed, objections to divisions of public funds have been so strong that the people of nearly all the states have approved amendments to state constitutions in order to remove the question from continual discussion. The movement for the adoption of constitutional amendments of this kind is still in progress. In Massachusetts in 1917 the people of that state went further than most states by adopting by a substantial majority a constitutional amendment which, with only one or two very minor exceptions, prohibits the expenditure of public money for the support of any institutions, or activities, that are not under full public control.

Maine, on the other hand, borrowed in 1820 the phrasing of the constitution in force at the time in the mother state, and has not on this point since amended it so as to forbid public financial support to private institutions. Hence that state, with a very few others, may still contribute public funds to the support of private schools, some of which retain their denominational affiliations.

The adoption of constitutional amendments and the enactment of statutes, however, have not wholly solved the problem of relationships of private education to the public treasury. There are various questions which continue to perplex not only communities but also some of the states. Recently there have been legal rulings and decisions which authorize the expenditure of public funds for health service of children attending parochial schools. Since these services are regarded as apart from education, prohibitory constitutional clauses are held not to apply. In some instances there have been other rulings and decisions which support the legality of spending public money for the transportation of children to private schools. This practice appears to many to imply indirect contributions, at least, of public money for the assistance of education of pupils in private schools. Very lately there has been injected into this financial phase of the matter still another consideration, namely the one as to whether or not allocations of federal funds to education within the states are subject to the limitations of state constitutions.

It may be well here to observe that constitutional enactments are at best only the indices of change and progress. They are not their primary causes. They record the direction in which public opinion goes and the distance it covers. They are imperatively important as regulatory mechanisms, but it is the force of public opinion that must make and keep them operative as mechanisms. Our people have had enough experience so that they ought to know that, either within or outside of legal controls, realistic performance does not always conform to the ideals set forth in constitutions and laws.

Hence it would be altogether too much to say that as a result of the various legal steps that have been taken, sectarianism has completely disappeared from the public schools. The forces of tradition and local sentiment have been and are too strong to have permitted any such outcome. There are communities, many of them, where denominational influence in the appointment of teachers is strong to the point of being compelling. Boards of education, controlled by local prejudices, refuse employment to Catholic, Jewish, or Protestant teachers as the case may be.

Teachers color their instruction in harmony with their own views or with those of the authorities or of the neighborhood. Jewish rabbis make the point that two distinctively Christian festivals, Easter and Christmas, with their influence on the faith of Jewish children, are almost universally observed in the public schools. Religious pictures hang on schoolroom walls. It is sometimes charged that textbooks carry sectarian implications. A teacher, merely for purposes of information (as she thinks), explains the significance of the Rosary. Clergymen, and others, are sometimes accused of giving more than a tinge of sectarianism to talks they give in the schools. In many communities the practice of holding baccalaureate and graduation exercises in any church is held to imply sectarian influence, and, on that ground, the practice is criticized or forbidden.

In sum, the impact of all these and other customs and practices is very considerable. What happens, of course, is that no objections are likely to be felt if the population of the community is exclusively of one faith. In other cases minorities sometimes seem to feel no special concern about the infringements, while in others they are disturbed but think it inexpedient to take steps to protect themselves. In rare cases appeals are made to higher authorities or to the courts. All of this is representative of the way in which the American people deal with realities, all the while they are holding more or less tenaciously to convictions and ideals. Whether in this case the progress towards the ideal has been as rapid as it ought to have been, the observation here is that granting that much ground must still be won, there has been substantial progress towards a divorce of sectarianism from American public education.

The use of the Bible has had a conspicuous place throughout the discussions about religion in the public schools. This issue, if not entirely removed from dispute, seems in most parts of the country to be approaching practical settlements. At least, it has come to the point where its legal status is fairly clear.

There is no state where by explicit provisions of law the Bible is excluded. Eleven states, on the other hand, have enacted statutes that require Bible reading, and six other states by legislative action permit but do not require it. In twenty states it has been ruled by departments of law or education that the Bible is not a sectarian book and thus, by implication, that it can be used in the public schools. In twelve states by official rulings or by common consent the use of the Bible is held to be not permissible.

Within these general directives, permissives, or prohibitions there is a considerable variance of practice. In most states there may be no comments on the reading. Interesting peculiarities among state laws are the following: In Pennsylvania "at least ten verses should be read . . . at the opening of each and every public school." In Idaho the prescription calls for reading "from ten to twenty verses," these to be selected from the "standard American version of the Bible." The selection of verses is left to the State Board of Education, but textual reading must be from the Book itself. Still further, in Idaho, a child who asks a question

about the reading is directed by the teacher to go to the
parent or guardian for an answer. In Massachusetts the law
expressly provides that, when the parent objects, a pupil
may not be required to take any personal part in the reading from any particular version of the Bible. In Tennessee,
teachers are directed by law "not to read the same chapter
more than twice within the same session." The members of
the Maine legislature went still further in guiding local
school committees and teachers by suggesting in the law
that in "readings from the Scripture" there be "special emphasis upon the Ten Commandments, the Psalms of David,
the Proverbs of Solomon, the Sermon on the Mount, and
the Lord's Prayer." These citations reflect the inclination
of legislatures to comply with public opinion as well as
their anxiety to keep clear of sectarian complications. A
vexing issue about the use of the Bible, current in some
places, relates to its use as a textbook in such subjects as literature, history, and philosophy. It is complained that bar-
ring the use of the Bible for such purposes is to deny to
youth one of the most remarkable of all source books. Yet,
in the view of some, lay teachers should not attempt inter-
pretations of the Book. It is objected that instruction about
the Bible for whatever purpose may, in effect, lead to sectarian indoctrination. On the other hand, teaching about
the Bible, even as literature or history, is open to obvious
criticisms if it is given by a clergyman.

However, it is incorrect to conclude that nothing about
the Bible, or its teachings, gets into the schools. The means
of its entrance are so numerous that in the final result public

school youth get no small amount of knowledge about the Bible. Ideas, ideals, and knowledge cannot be completely barred by walls or statutes.

It is significant that the exclusion of the Bible from the schools, and limitations of the extent of its use, are not the results of objections raised by "materialists" or agnostics. They arise from the contentions of the various sects. Hence the hope of wider uses of the Bible rests upon whatever progress towards agreements the several denominations can make.

*what is being done as a solution*

### III

A movement of the past twenty-five years that has recently made considerable progress is one which aims to enlist the coöperation of the public schools and the churches by means of a formula called "released time." While this plan has the enthusiastic support of some churches and the endorsement of many school authorities, it has implications of the revival of sectarian issues.

Briefly the essential feature of this plan is the excusing of pupils, by consent of their parents, from a part of the required public school attendance period with the understanding that the time thus "released" is to be used in weekday religious teaching.

The churches, usually through councils, agree to provide instruction in religion while the school authorities agree to give to the churches a certain amount of the time that otherwise the children would spend in school. This seems to be an exchange between the government and the churches under the terms of which the former contributes compulsory school time while the latter contribute denominational instruction.

There are variations of detail in the manner in which "released time" is administered. Usually the period is for one hour of each week. A council of churches, or some similar organization, is likely to be designated as the authority for seeing that the churches meet their part of the agreement. The religious instruction is in most cases conducted in the churches of the several denominations. Schoolrooms or school buildings have rarely been used. In some cities, credits of achievement in religious instruction on "released time" may be transferred to the public school record of the child. Here are some important questions. One of these relates to the propriety of accepting, for public school records, the results of tests covering doctrinal teaching. There is also the question here of the legality of the approval by public school authorities of instruction conducted by non-certificated or unauthorized teachers. Most states require that teachers hold credentials showing their qualifications in the various subjects they are expected to teach. It is difficult to see how public school authorities can justify the acceptance of credits for instruction given by teachers who do not hold the required state certificates. Teachers of other subjects would not be permitted under the laws of most states to enjoy this exceptional privilege.

In a bulletin of the Federal Office of Education issued in 1941, it was reported that the "released time" plan was in operation in 488 systems in thirty-eight states. The number of school systems in each state ranged from 1 to 5 among sixteen states to the highest, 101, in the case of New York. Of the 488 school systems reporting, 357 state that the average attendance in week-day classes was 164,013. Of this number, about four-fifths were elementary school children and one-fifth were youth of secondary school age. Since the bulletin was issued favorable action has been taken by a number of additional school systems so that the total number of pupils enrolled has no doubt very considerably increased.

To illustrate the principles underlying the plan, it may be useful to refer to Maine, where the legislature has by statutory enactment legalized the practice of dismissing pupils for religious instruction in the churches. The law of Maine bears the title "An Act to Provide Moral Instruction for Children in Connection with the Public Schools." The theme of this title is further emphasized in the first section of the Act which states that "school committees are authorized to provide for the moral instruction of pupils in the manner provided by the Act." Here is evidence of the continuing view that moral instruction derives from the teaching of religion.

The Maine law further provides that the school committee may "authorize and complete a survey of the religious affiliation of all pupils attending the public schools, and ascertain those pupils who desire and have the consent of parent or guardian for moral instruction." Probably the proponents of this particular measure did not really intend to urge this unusual extension of the authority of school committees which gives to them the right to inquire into the religious affiliations of public school pupils.

The Maine law still further authorizes school committees "to make arrangements with the respective persons in charge of the several denominations" for carrying out the provisions of the Act. Here is apparently an indication of an attempt to effect a local union of government and church in sectarian education. A particularly significant implication of this law is to be found in the following clause: "Any child who fails to receive the aforesaid moral instruction shall remain in school during the period when such instruction is being given . . . but . . . such child so remaining shall not receive any educational advantages over the children receiving said moral instruction." A child who is not out of school on "released time" is thus evidently in the unhappy situation of being compelled to stay in school during "released time" but without receiving, during that period, either moral instruction or educational gain!

In one city of a mid-western state the formula of "released time" has been applied for more than twenty years to the expressed satisfaction of the school authorities, the churches, and presumably a majority of the citizens. The Federation of Churches of the city issues a circular bearing the slogan "If We Enlarge the Head but Shrink the Heart, What Value All Our Education?" This repeats the old charge that American public schools are interested chiefly in the intellectual development of children, disregarding their moral growth. Besides, the implication is that the lack must be supplied by the churches, presumably through the doctrinal teachings of each. An accompanying circular issued by the Federation states, among others, the following advantages of the week-day church schools: "An equality of religious experience for all children," "an interdenominational experience in religion (which builds tolerance and understanding of all religions and faiths)," "an experience in ecumenicity for our city (a Protestant unity)," "Christian education for the unchurched (helping these unreached to find Sunday Church Schools)," and "religious instruction in connection with public school education." An analysis of these advantages would seem to indicate that the equality of religious experience can hardly extend to those children who are not "released" from school. Other questions may be raised; for example, whether religious instruction in connection with public schools can properly be directed toward producing "Protestant unity" and whether or not the churches are justified in making indirect use of the public school system for reaching the unchurched. It may be doubted whether the formula as applied in the city in question, and for the objectives named, could be generally applied without producing serious disunity, not to mention the still unresolved doubt as to whether these practices violate the principle of non-sectarianism in public education.

Although these plans for giving religious instruction on "released time" have been approved by many thoughtful and well-meaning people and have been given the sanction of both legal and educational advisers, it is impossible to avoid the impression that they represent, in essence, another attempt to join church and state for the promotion of sectarian education.

It should be noted that the sponsors of this plan have insisted upon having released some of the time set aside by law to be used for the purpose of public education. They have not looked with favor on the alternative arrangement by which the schools would be closed for all pupils for a certain period each week leaving parents at complete liberty to assume responsibility for whatever use of this time they might elect. The sponsors of "released time" insist that children not excused for sectarian instruction be kept in school. Obviously there is here an added incentive or pressure for children to attend church classes. Thus the "released time" element of the scheme seems to be for making use of compulsory attendance laws to encourage, if not to enforce, participation in sectarian teaching.

There are certain principles that are basic to the American theory of public education. It is believed that it is a unifying, not a divisive agency, that it does not raise with children questions of difference of race and creed, and that it is in the service of all the people without discrimination in favor of any. It may not prove to be wise to depart from these principles even for an hour each week.

IV

Practices in the colleges and universities in the use of the Bible and the teaching of religion differ greatly from those which have appeared in the lower schools.

American colleges, in regard to their support and control, are of three quite distinct classifications. First there are those institutions that are maintained by the several religious denominations; second the independent or liberal arts colleges, some of which were once but are no longer under denominational patronage; and third, the publicly financed and administered municipal and state colleges and universities.

In the colleges of the first group the teaching of religion is, of course, given a prominent place. Creed and articles of faith are likely to be emphasized. Indoctrination into the tenets of the supporting church is to be expected.

In the colleges of the second group courses in Bible study and religion are commonly offered, but are usually not required. Courses in Bible study are often found in departments of English, while those in religion may be allocated to the departments of philosophy.

It is perhaps popularly assumed that the public institutions of higher education give little or no recognition to the kinds of religious activity that are common to the colleges of the first and second groups. As a matter of fact this popular assumption is not a correct one.

A recent examination of the current catalogues of forty-eight of the publicly supported state colleges and universities reveals that in them are made available religious activities neither greatly dissimilar in kind nor less in number than they are in the "independent" colleges.

It would be interesting to speculate on the reasons why practices not acceptable to the public in their lower schools

have apparently been admitted more freely to their higher
institutions. Perhaps the incidence of federal funds, which
are not subject to narrow constitutional limitations about
their use in denominational schools, may have something to
do with it. Perhaps a recognition of the maturity of the students may modify parental and church resistance to their
participation in religious discussions. Perhaps the views of
college students themselves have been a factor. Or perhaps
most likely, it is recognized that at this level of education
there is no area whatever of human concern that can be
kept outside the bounds of examination and study.

In the forty-eight institutions that were lately sampled
there are student assemblies, convocations, and general exercises of one kind or another which definitely reflect religious idealism. In nearly all of them there are faculty and
student clubs and organizations that are religious both in
name and in declared purpose. Some of these clubs are denominational in character, bearing titles that are associated
with the Protestant, Catholic, and Jewish faiths. That these
clubs provide suitable opportunity for the uniting of students of similar religious beliefs and convictions there can
be no doubt. They are effective, too, in preserving for college youth some of the church associations they had en-
joyed in their own homes and communities.

In the listed offerings of these forty-eight publicly supported institutions there is good evidence that their authorities believe it to be suitable to add to these somewhat
extra-curricular activities opportunities for the formal
study of the Bible and religion.

The classification of these course offerings varies, the auspices under which they are taught differ, and in other respects there are certain distinguishing details. The central purposes, however, seem to be alike. They reflect an explicit intention to meet the expectation of students and the public for something that may be accepted as "religious education." In some cases a good deal of caution is shown in the administration of the courses with the intention of avoiding legal complications.

Of the entire forty-eight institutions only eight report that there are no formal courses in the study of the Bible or religion. Of the remaining forty colleges, eleven list courses in religion, twenty in Bible study, while nine of them offer courses in both the Bible and religion. Courses in these subjects are variously allocated, some of them to departments of religion, others to departments of English or philosophy.

Brief abstracts of course descriptions may suggest what the authorities conceive to be the character and purposes of the several courses.

Descriptive of those on the Bible as literature are the following: "Survey of types of literature in the books of the Bible; influence of the Bible on modern literature." "Study of King James version of the Bible as a masterpiece of world literature and an English classic."

There are some course descriptions that reflect the intention to open for treatment some of the issues with which the modern church is concerned. Illustrative of these is: "A psychological and historical study of religion followed by a survey of some of its philosophical implications." A course in "Non-sectarian study of western religious philosophies" obviously suggests that students are to be invited to an impartial examination of faiths not their own.

The following titles and descriptions are likewise significant of the character of the studies presented to students: "Modern social problems of christianity—study of social and moral principles in modern civilization; Religion in modern life—basic questions such as the validity of religious experience and the efficacy of prayer; The life and teaching of Jesus—study of life, work, teaching, and significance of Jesus; Educational work of the church—course designed to help lay foundations for leadership of educational groupings within the church."

An interesting attempt to provide a balance of treatment of the three divisions of religion most prominent in American communities is indicated in the case of one university which offers, among several courses, the following: "The life and teaching of Jesus—systematic presentation of the teaching of Jesus which relates to the religious values of the writings of the prophets with reference to social teachings; Jewish history—spiritual contributions and social, economic, and cultural life of the Jewish people; The history and influence of the Catholic Church—growth, influence, contribution, and function in realm of modern affairs." "These courses," the catalogue takes pains to announce, "in the history and articles of belief of the three major western faiths are given by the respective Counselors in Religion, or others, designated by the churches represented. They are independent of University supervision and control although the facilities of the University are available as for other courses. Students register for these courses at the regular registration period and may do so in addition to a normal semester load." This statement indicates that the courses are probably given without academic credit.

The University of Kansas, announcing sixteen courses within the field of religion and one other course in the study of the Bible (listed in the department of philosophy), is among the institutions which offer the largest number of courses in religion. These courses, however, while listed in the catalogue, are offered in a separate "School of Religion" which the catalogue explains is "not an organic part of the university" although enrollment is effected in the same way as for other university courses and credit within certain described limits may be allowed. Similar arrangements for teaching courses in religion for whose administration and teaching the authorities apparently do not take responsibility are made by other universities. The Bible School of Missouri, for example, sponsors certain courses in religion for which the University of Missouri gives credit for as many as fourteen hours towards the degree of Bachelor of Arts. In similar fashion, the Montana School of Religion, organized by a committee representing the university and several religious denominations, makes available to their students five courses that are classified under "religion." The Fargo School of Religious Education, in connection with North Dakota Agricultural College, provides another illustration of this informal type of contract between a state college and an outside agency or association. This School is described as being under the control of an independent board of citizens from the town, drawn from all religious faiths and providing courses that are supported entirely by voluntary contributions.

The fourteen courses listed in this School indicate a wide range of interest in or interpretation of, religious education. Among them are: "Introduction to religion, teachings of Jesus, early Hebrew history, Christian character education, and moral laws." The intention to give breadth of treatment in teaching of religion is also shown in the case of this School by such a course as "Comparative religion—a study of the fundamental beliefs, doctrines, and ideals of the important religions of the world." This same intention of giving breadth of treatment to the teaching of religion is indicated in another college by the following: "Living religions of the Orient, a course which invites the study of Islam, Hinduism, Buddhism, and other faiths."

Courses designed to deal with the much-debated topic of "Religion and Science" appear in several catalogues. Illustrative of these is: "Science and religion," which is described as aiming to show that both religious faith and scientific research may work harmoniously in helping students to understand their relationship to a supreme purpose.

In connection with one publicly supported institution of higher learning there are two "Institutes" which provide registration and courses that are offered without charge to any regularly matriculated student of the university. Under certain conditions, a student may elect a total of eight credits for courses thus taken.

As in the case of the "independent" colleges, courses in Bible and religion in public institutions are invariably elective. There are no figures available to indicate how many students in these state colleges elect courses of these kinds. It is probable that the proportion to the total enrollment is not large.

One thing seems to be quite apparent on the evidence of the catalogues, namely, that denominationalism or sectarianism seems to play a minor part in religious education in state universities and colleges. Since that is the case, it may perhaps be not unreasonable to expect that these college students, representative of higher education, may exercise a not inconsiderable influence in bringing about a more intelligent and sympathetic understanding of the objectives of the churches and the ideals of religion.

### V

How then, in this atmosphere of discussion, negation, experimentation, and confusion, can it be said that the American people have been determined to keep religion in the schools? The very conditions mentioned, almost, if not quite, prove the point. The preventive measures that have been taken have been clearly directed to bar sectarianism and not to ban religion. If religion can be in the schools only in terms of creeds and articles of faith, clearly enough religion can find no place in the public schools. On the other hand, if religion be interpreted in broader terms than those of creed, then religion is not only in the schools, it also permeates them.

Public schools are not isolated from society nor are they insulated against the currents that flow through it. The philosophies that pervade the social structure probably find clearer and more dynamic expression in the schools than in any other institution. This is the case because of the nature of education, the atmosphere and environment of the classroom, the predominance of youth, and, by no means least, the constant guidance of teachers. The very objectives and methods of education as found and practiced in the schools reflect basic religious philosophies. In recent years increasingly, the sanctity of the individual with all his rights and needs has been advancing to first place in the respect of educators. The substance and methods of education are more and more reflecting concern about moral, physical, intellectual, and spiritual development. That behavior is evidence that morality is a cardinal principle of public education. Since both religion as increasingly interpreted and education as increasingly practiced are mutually involved in the development of character as reflected in behavior, it is inevitable that both precept and performance should become more and more the substance of education. Viewed thus, there is indeed much evidence to show that the schools, so far from being "non-religious" are, as a matter of fact, extremely effective for translating religious philosophies into decent individual and social behavior.

In a recent letter, Brigadier General Farrand Sayre (ret.) writes: "If I were an Army chaplain I would discuss honesty, honor, loyalty, duty, justice, mercy, and coöperation. A study of these words will improve our knowledge of our relations with one another; and since the ideas suggested by them are inspired by the Spirit of God, they lead also to a knowledge of Him." What is true of the Army in this admirable statement can be applied to the schools. They not only teach the virtues that are inherent and stressed in religion; they likewise provide an infinite number of opportunities for their practice.

Formal instruction in religion has long been required in the schools of most European countries. Formal instruction in religion has not been required in the public schools of the United States. A comparison of the results reveals no substantial proof that the American policy has either destroyed or perverted the essential goals towards which religion, in its broader and best sense, leads.

HOWARD MUMFORD JONES

‣*3*‣

# Religious Education in the State Universities

THE problem of American religious education is no-
where more complicated than in the state-supported
colleges and universities. No thoroughly satisfactory solution of the question has been found; and although nobody is happy about the existing state of affairs, nobody
seems to know what is to be done next. Part of the reason
for the dilemma is historic, part of it is the trial-and-error
method of seeking a solution. Possibly the elements which
make up the problem are essentially so inharmonious that
they can never be reconciled.

The impulses which led to the creation of American
state universities derive from the eighteenth century and
partake of its rationalism. Even if those who created these
institutions were not deists, they were children of an age
when denominational lines had softened in a nation that
was predominantly Protestant. Roman Catholic author-
itarianism had lost some of its rigor under the genial sun of

the Enlightenment; and anyway, there were not enough members of this faith in the little republic to complicate the problem. The most characteristic product of the Enlightenment among American state universities was of course the University of Virginia, to which Jefferson, whom his enemies called an immoral atheist and who was in fact a benevolent deist, gave at its founding a strongly agnostic bias, excluding both ecclesiastical establishments and the clergy from its body. The exclusion was in no sense permanent; and it is interesting and important to note that other Southern state universities, which on paper at least were created at the end of the eighteenth century,[1] came into being after the excesses of the French Revolution had created a strong religious counter-movement in the United States. Caught in this counter-current, these struggling "universities" lost whatever agnostic characteristics they had originally possessed and were in fact, if not in law, managed by one or another of the Protestant denominations dominant in the South. Thus strained relations between the Presbyterian clergy and President Thomas Cooper eventually led to that worthy's resignation as president of South Carolina College (Cooper was a Unitarian who once predicted the eventual triumph of a materialistic philosophy); and Methodists, Baptists, Presbyterians, and Episcopalians

[1] The University of North Carolina was provided for in the new constitution of 1776, chartered in 1785, and opened in 1795; the University of Georgia was chartered in 1785 and opened in 1801; the College of South Carolina, which was to become the University of South Carolina, was chartered in 1801 and opened in 1805.

fought each other for the control of the University of Georgia.

The great Middle Western universities characteristically came into being during the height of Victorian rationalism and the enthusiasm for the state-supported German university. Thus the ground for the creation of the University of Michigan in 1837 was prepared by an interest in Cousin's report on the Prussian educational system, and Tappan, the first effective head of that institution, was so enthusiastic a believer in *Lehrfreiheit* and *Lehrnfreiheit* that he advanced beyond the ability of his board of regents to follow him and was forced to resign. The development of the University of Wisconsin (opened in 1849) was likewise strongly influenced by a concept of social utility which owed something to Jeremy Bentham and the notion of a state-supported system of education, European in its origins. That relations between the "godless" university and religious denominations were sometimes tense in the Middle West is undeniable, but a habit of securing presidents and professors from denominational colleges in the East, a decline of militancy among rationalists, and a gradual acceptance among scientists of the pleasant fiction that the research-worker merely thinks God's thoughts after him did much to diminish antagonisms.

The Civil War damaged state-supported education North and South as wars always do, and the religious reaction which followed the conflict was no sooner launched than the great Darwinian controversy swirled through pulpit and lecture hall. In a loose sense of the term the conflict was over Darwin's theory; more particularly it would appear that Huxley's famous lecture-essay on "The Physical Basis of Life" focussed attention upon the inherent discrepancy between agnosticism and revealed religion. In the South the state universities were still too feeble to be immediately affected; in the North the passage of the Morrill Act in 1862 had the effect of strengthening the appeal of science because it put science at work in the service of the state. On the whole therefore fundamentalist attempts to capture the "godless" state university were turned aside in the North. In the South the conflict came later; and the anti-evolution bills, which were occasionally passed, illustrated the fears of Protestant denominations that state universities would get out of hand.

Although the American state university owes much of its theory and practice to the university concept in nineteenth-century Germany, one important differentiation must be made. In German universities the theological faculty played an important part, theology being considered as much an object of exact study as chemistry or Latin. Under American constitutional theory this was impossible, inasmuch as a strict construction of the doctrine that church and state are separate, means that the state university is forever debarred from supporting a school of theology. Practical political experience buttresses political theory, as the squabbles to control Southern state universities in the earlier part of the last century sadly illustrate.

But theology, though it is shut out at the door, creeps in

at the window. The professor of philosophy and the professor of literature can scarcely fail to discuss some of the great theological systems of mankind. The professor of history, European or American, must perforce deal with Catholic dogma, the rationale of the Reformation, and the story of Greek Orthodox faith. The scientific lecturer, by the very assumptions he is compelled to make, frequently disturbs the naïf religious beliefs of youngsters out of high school and, indirectly, of their parents. Moreover, there seems to be no prohibition against supporting professorships of Oriental lore, whose specialty may be Buddhism or some other religious faith of the Ancient East. In the state university religious faiths can thus be studied and "taught" indirectly (or directly, if their American following is negligible), but they cannot be directly "taught" or, what is more to the point, directly defended against indirect assault. A sincere Christian or a Jew has in this sense a legitimate complaint against an educational institution which omits from an all-embracing curriculum that religious faith which he thinks the greatest thing in life, and certainly one of the potent forces in shaping education.

The state university, on the other hand, has also its unanswerable argument. Even if the constitutional prohibition could be waived, what sort of theology, what kind or kinds of religious instruction should be offered? Obviously it cannot be that of any single church, inasmuch as the state university belongs to the whole people and not to any sect among them. It cannot support as many chairs of theology as there are principal denominations in the state, even supposing that a church like the Roman Catholic would agree to this practice, because the university must control appointments to its faculty, and there is no very good way by which a theoretically impartial body like the state university and a sectarian body like a church can agree upon governing principles in this situation. Infinite difficulties of budgets, library appropriations, student hours, required and permissive courses, differences in interpretation of the Sabbath, and relations with other non-religious chairs would arise. The state university is sincerely anxious not to commit itself to any sectarian doctrine, including agnosticism and atheism; but it is also sincerely anxious not to omit so large a part of life as religion represents, and so the dilemma increases.

No solution, as I have said, is satisfactory because in some sense the quarrel is as ancient as the struggle over the investitures or the various concordats which have marked European attempts to reconcile irreconcilables. For in the state university the state confronts religious denominations which, being evangelical bodies, must essentially desire to control the state, including the state university, however politely this desire is masked. Indeed, if they are true to themselves, these religious bodies must desiderate the time when all men shall see the truth as it is revealed to the denomination in question—and what better time to drive home this point than in the malleable years of youth? And why let "godless" professors have the whole charge of these formative years?

Practical compromises are worked out, often under the

convenient ambiguity of the word "religion." For if the state university be prohibited from maintaining a faculty of theology, courses in "comparative religion" compromise nobody, commit nobody, and perhaps make for general good will—albeit instruction in "comparative religion" has here and there stirred up the very difficulty it was supposed to alleviate. Such courses may be given by a discreet professor of ethics or a philosopher; they may appear in the offerings of the department of history or of anthropology; sometimes they even appear, disguised, in the English department as "The Bible as Literature," "The Great Bibles of Mankind," or something similar. Similarly, courses not so named, in ethics, sociology, social problems, or literature, may be quietly understood to deal with the problem of "religion." In an unobtrusive way these courses often do an immense amount of good in two directions: they help puzzled undergraduates and they reassure the churches that the university is not a hotbed of "atheism." But of course "religion" taught comparatively is religion on an objective or impersonal basis and does not necessarily lead to that direct influence upon conduct and thought which many denominations desire to exercise.

A second device is the maintenance of a "religious counsellor" at the expense of the state, wholly or in part: Such an official, presumably kindly and impartial, serves as a liaison officer between the university and the denominations. His is the office through which the local pastor, priest, or rabbi may secure information about the religious preferences of students and arrange meetings for them, welcome them to their temporary church home in the university community, help them in need, and employ them in good works if they are willing. Sometimes such a counsellor will arrange lectures of a quasi-denominational sort, or even a "religious week," though to do so trespasses upon the impartial attitude of the university and may arouse denominational resentment. And of course such an officer serves to guide the various student religious organizations, such as the Y.M. C.A., the Y.W.C.A., the Newman Club, the Menorah Society, and the like. If the university include a considerable number of students from abroad, he may assist these to find a "church home."

The theoretical reason for his existence is also that the puzzled undergraduate from a devout home, confronting in the university for the first time some of the ancient dilemmas of knowledge versus faith, may come to the religious counsellor for wise guidance. In this sense the religious counsellor absorbs some of the functions elsewhere characteristic of the "university" Y.M.C.A. secretary or of the dean of students, dean of men, or psychiatrist; and in this sense the counsellor is supposed to be chosen for his understanding of student psychology. One should not indict a whole profession, and there are occasional men who have been successful in what is at best a very difficult task. But on the whole it cannot be said that undergraduates characteristically take their troubles to the religious counsellor. To begin with, the counsellor has to be all things to all men— to be, in other words, strictly impartial among Catholics, Protestants, Jews, agnostics, and all the rest. This is in itself an impossible assignment. In the next place, even if he is impartial, the best he can do is to canalize the problem with all of its emotional overtones in the direction of the student's church, and yet it is sometimes this very minister that the student is trying to get away from. And finally it must be gently said that in a faculty of experts the religious counsellor fares badly because the philosophic and scientific competition is very great, and up to now his job has attracted few persons of outstanding genius. The puzzled undergraduate, if he goes to an adult at all, is therefore far more likely to confide in a sympathetic member of the faculty.

These are two principal ways in which the university has tried to solve the problem. The denominations have also made friendly approaches. Characteristic is the assignment to the nearest local church or synagogue of a "student pastor"; the building, if means permit, of student dormitories, houses, or club-houses; or, if such a single building is beyond the capacity of a given denomination, the sharing of such enterprises with others. Social groups are organized, some attempt is made to introduce the lonely undergraduate into the homes of church members, and the church life of the student is thoughtfully looked after. But this would happen, so to speak, if there were no university, and scarcely meets the intellectual problem of religious instruction. Therefore the churches have tried a second scheme.

Adjoining the campuses of many state universities, particularly in the South, one will find one or more buildings housing a so-called Bible chair or chairs. This means that the denomination in question supports a teacher of its own faith who offers in a building owned or rented by his denomination instruction in the Bible, in theology, or in "religion," sufficiently mature in character as to challenge the interests of undergraduate and to compete on an intellectual level with the courses offered in the university. These courses are mostly extra-curricular in nature, and it is a tribute to the earnestness with which they are taught and to a quality of soul-searching among undergraduates that they continue to survive, even where no college credit is given for them.

Sooner or later, however, demand is made that these well-intentioned courses shall be credited as part of the regular baccalaureate work. On the part of the denomination various moves are made. It offers to allow the university to share in the appointment of a teacher. It offers to contribute to the expenses incidental to the situation. It offers to allow the university authorities to inspect the instruction and to refuse credit if it sinks below par. It offers to have the work graded on a proper university scale, to meet minimum requirements in written work, number of books assigned, etc., etc. It even offers to make efforts towards liaison with the department of philosophy, the relevant sciences, literary courses, etc. And if these demands are not met, it must be bluntly said of some localities that veiled threats are issued against the university—the right-thinking people of the state will see to it that the appropriations for supporting this worldly institution are curtailed, and so on. To the credit of most denominations it should be stated that threats like these are felt to be unChristian, and that, when they are made, they originate not with the thoughtful leaders of the church in question, but with political aspirants eager to play up to the incipient anti-intellectualism which is as much a part of the American commonwealth as is its generous support of education.

Universities have yielded here and there, appointed a faculty committee to "control" these Bible courses, and hoped for the best. The good that lies in such instruction obviously cannot be laughed away by the most fanatical secularist. It is also probable that, however mediocre the intellectual standards of such courses may prove to be, the college of arts will contain legitimate courses no better in quality and no more demanding. Finally, it is not cynical to observe mildly that the acceptance of such work by the university college of arts has often proved a political convenience in dealing with legislative committees of fundamentalist views.

On the whole, however, the universities have rejected the claims of the Bible chairs to be counted equal to the departments in the regular faculty. In the first place, if denominations A, B, and C establish intellectually reputable chairs, it does not follow that denominations E, F, and G will do so; and yet these weaker brethren may reasonably say that if the first three denominations have a right to retain control of their students to this extent, the same right cannot be withheld from *them.* As for "standards," who, in a faculty or out of it, ever admits he teaches a snap course? In the second place, difficulties about texts arise: what is

felt to be the right level of theological difficulty for the
Roman Catholic seems too high or too low for the Baptist;
the Jewish body is, theologically speaking, in so different a
category from the Episcopalians as to make a common denominator of difficulty hard to find; and smaller sects, or
sects with a small number of student followers, are deprived
of any instruction whatsoever. In the third place, conflicts
between the theologians and the rest of the faculty inevitably arise—over evolution, over science, over pragmatism,
over laboratory methods in ethics or psychology, over the
interpretation of literary masterpieces; and the difference
between these troubles and the inevitable quarrels between
learned men in the universities and simple men outside the
universities is that the representatives of the Bible chairs
are neither in nor out, but occupy an ambiguous and embar-
rassing position. From the point of view of the regular
faculty they are interlopers to be suffered and kept down;
from the point of view of the denominations, they represent
the university faculty or, if not, represent the denomination in the faculty. And finally it must be confessed that
shrewd students shop around among these courses, much as,
in earlier years, they shopped around among Sunday
schools looking for the most promising Christmas tree. It
must be clear from this simple and unsatisfactory analysis,
therefore, that the university has in fact little effective
control over courses of this character, that good will is not
a proper substitute for intellectual rigor, and that in the
long run this solution of the problem raises more questions
than it settles.

What, then, is the answer? As I earlier indicated, the problem offers no eternally correct solution. The Roman Catholics believe that education is a function of the church, and put up with the presence of students of their faith in the state universities largely because they must. Obviously, therefore, they cannot acquiesce in the positivistic approach of the modern state university towards many problems— birth control as a sociological issue is such a one—on which that church has announced, or seems to have announced, a decision. Members of the Jewish faith are in the fortunate position of not being characteristically a proselytizing group; they are in the less fortunate position of having group solidarity thrust upon them. Like the Roman Catholics therefore they stand a little apart from other denominations. And the Protestant churches range from the cultured acceptance of the university world by the Episcopalians to the suspiciousness of other sects that shall here be nameless.

The common ground on which these churches and the university can, and do, most easily agree is some form of social work in the university community and some form of united front in social and international affairs. The fact that university students serve in settlement houses, legal aid institutes, scout groups, classes in English or citizenship for foreigners, and similar altruistic enterprises is a tribute to the social effectiveness of that fraternalism which is the better human part of religions. Equally a tribute is the vigorous expression of opinion by American undergraduates in state universities against racial discrimination and other evils. No university but will allow any undergraduate group of worthy purpose to meet in its buildings; out of such meetings, whatever the faith represented, have come frequent and effective contributions to academic opinion.

So far as the intellectual rigors of theology are concerned, of course, the state universities have nothing to offer. Indeed, they ought not offer anything here. So far as approving or disapproving any religious movement, church, sect, creed, or denomination is concerned, their stand must be neutral. This neutrality, to be sure, exposes them to gross misinterpretation. To many simple men any state university is a nest of godless sinners. This caricature is, of course, as wide of the truth as the cartoon cherished by a few university professors, to the effect that churches are the eternal enemy of intellectual progress.

Indirectly, however, the state universities probably accomplish more for religious education than the Bible chairs are prepared to admit. To be sure, something depends upon what one means by "religion," but over and beyond the pragmatic social services discussed above, the universities, in sheer self-preservation, must judge the contributions of the churches with an affirmative tolerance, however critical that tolerance may *in extremis* prove to be. The thoughtful historical study of what churches have been and done may, indeed, lead to scepticism; it is more likely to lead to that intellectual humility which is the beginning of wisdom. In history, man's inhumanity to man may be the beginning of the search for God.

On the other hand, the university trains its students to

higher intellectual expectations than the average church, the average minister, can satisfy. After being lectured to by expert men, however dull these men may be, the student is likely to find the ordinary sermon, Catholic, Protestant, or Jewish, singularly unsatisfactory. After training by professional thinkers, the vague good will of the Sunday-school superintendent is less than the dust. It is not the university, but the churches that must become intellectually alive if they are to retain the allegiance of graduates from state-supported institutions of higher learning in the United States. Single ministers and single churches see this; it must be confessed that the majority of churches do not. The consequence is that the state university student who is looking for religious education at least as good as the secular training he receives from an expert faculty concludes that whatever else it may be, religious education offers no challenge to the mind. It ought to. But does it?

Victor L. Butterfield

+ *4* +

# *Religion in the Liberal College*

B EHIND the immediate concerns and comforts of life
there always lurks the ultimate mystery of things. Men
can, and do, live as animals, going about their foraging,
procreating, and quarreling, or settling down to their crea-
ture comforts before the fire when the stomach is full,
the pantry stocked, and their neighbor asleep. But men can
and do find more in life than this. A restlessness of the heart,
a questioning of the mind, a lighting of the fancy, a compulsion of the conscience, and a transport of the spirit,
these forever bestir the human animal and urge him toward
the aspirations and achievements we call civilized. Questions
of what we are and visions of what we might be carry him
beyond the body and the day, and confront him with the
infinite cosmos, its endlessness of time and space, of fact
and event, its order and conflict, its hospitality and cruelty
to the human species, and men's even greater hospitality
and cruelty to one another. Thus arise the great eternal
problems of man at his best, and thus are born the

highest of man's achievements. Out of these the quality of happiness and sorrow has risen and spread, despite the ebb tide of the animal pull. As these eternal problems are more widely faced and as the achievements which match them are more fully accomplished, civilization is maintained and increased. The tug is slow and hard; the counter-tugs and relapses are painful and disrupting. The battle rests on hope, on faith, and on the achievement and dynamic of human aspiration, intellectual and emotional, social, moral, and spiritual.

This is the basic hope and faith and aspiration that support the liberal college and the church. It is because of their great part in the battle that the college and religion are important. We are now passing through the greatest anguish that historic society has known. Much of what we mean by civilization has been strained, mangled, or destroyed. We are driven, therefore, to regain our losses on every front of human enterprise and to carry our efforts again and forever toward the eternal frontiers. To what degree and in what ways can religion and liberal learning unite in the offensive?

That is the problem with which we are here faced. Both religion and liberal learning are concerned with the personal and social destiny, and triumph, of man. This is their basic mutual concern. Beyond this their aims and methods have much in common, but they also differ. Only as we appreciate these similarities and differences, in both their ideal and actual manifestations, are we in a position to see the place of religion in the liberal college and to suggest methods for enriching and vitalizing the contributions of both to the high achievements of civilized and civilizing men.

I shall first make bold, therefore, to define what I conceive to be the ideal aims and basic methods of the liberal college on the one hand and of what I should call "high" religion on the other. I speak of high religion as that religion which is fundamentally commensurate, in varying degrees and combinations, with the other great human enterprises and insights. I speak, in other words, of that type of religion which, in various forms, can and often does consistently permeate or crown the lives of cultivated and sensitive men.

The basic purpose of the college is the promotion of liberal wisdom, the development in man of those powers and sensitivities which enable him to judge and desire what is true and good and beautiful, and to select the means for their attainment in the ways, and to the degrees, and in the proportions that his own experience and judgment decide, under the circumstances of his nature and of the world he finds about him. The faith of the college lies in the conviction that as a man seeks this wisdom, he finds it, and as he finds it, he reaps its intrinsic and its consequential rewards, both of which are high and abiding. Its faith further lies in the belief that, as greater numbers of men pursue this wisdom, its ferments spread strength, harmony, and great achievement in the society of men.

There are three fundamental methods of achieving the liberal ideal. The first is the method of options, the urging of a multitude and variety of answers to the questions with which life and the cosmos present us, answers which constitute genuine possibilities for choice, that give us positive possibilities for significant enterprise and its attendant happiness. The second fundamental method is that already suggested, the autonomy of the individual concerned in the selection of the options explored. His judgment, his experience, his aspiration, do the choosing. Thirdly, the liberal ideal emphasizes the method of knowledge and reason. It is through a knowledge of men and their world, through the hard exercise of reason, through the exploration and reflection of the mind that the spirit is sensitized and that man discovers those truths and values that make for the deepest and most abiding satisfactions and the richest social concords. Thus through knowledge of fact and of the "best that has been said," through a capacity to handle the ideas involved in these or the principles derived from them, through an appreciation of the achievements of men in many of the great areas of cultural experience, through the solidity of reason, the spontaneity of imagination, the sympathy of insight, the flight of inspiration—through these the liberal college believes men can be trained with minds so rich, so sensitive, so versatile, so profound, that they can most successfully meet by positive achievement the critical and unpredictable problems of life, be they personal or social, practical or theoretical, psychological or ethical, mundane or religious.

The college furthermore asks, beyond the common decencies, for those virtues which are basic to its enterprise as a community devoted to this purpose—intellectual humility and integrity, mutual effort and a sense of common purpose, as well as respect and concern for the truths or opinions of others who are also searching man and his universe for answers.

What by comparison are the function and method of religion, ideally conceived? Not any particular religion, least of all sectarian orthodoxies, but universal religion or "high" religion, as it were, that basic attitude and enterprise of the spirit which in varying manifestations is commensurate with, and indeed may be integral to, most of the great cultural achievements of man.

Such religion has an intimate community with liberal learning and is one of its great options. Like art, like science, like philosophy, it is a focus of genuine possibility for human solutions and civilizing attainment. As *one* of the great areas of human spiritual achievement, however, it must perforce demand of its votaries some shift of emphasis within the frame of the liberal ideal. *Any* particular area of achievement or any philosophy of life requires such emphasis. A philosophy of life means in fact the selection and organized emphasis of values and principles to guide us in the business of living. But emphasis in one direction means de-emphasis in another. The life of science throws its weight more heavily on the principles of hypothesis, tangible evidence, experiment, detached appraisal. The life of art lives more dependently on the sense, on feeling, on creative enterprise, on transport. This is not to say that science can dispense in the proper degrees or places with creative imagination or the zest of sentiment, or that the life of art can similarly completely forego the evidence or detachment of science.

We are involved here in the varying balances of various comprehensive and interwoven patterns of many common elements.

Religion, therefore, also tends to throw its balance in one direction rather than another, and for religion it is in the direction of immediate concern with the problems of man and his relation to his universe. It is a conscious and deliberate quest for the underlying realities that inhere in or govern the cosmos, and for the demands they make on man if he is to achieve the harmony with life and destiny which is his ultimate concern. Hence the usual preoccupation of religion is with the search for God and the discovery of his nature, with the ultimate problem of good and evil, of freedom, tragedy, and triumph, with the human actions and attitudes that further the search and achieve the triumph.

These concerns are the emphatic ones, the nuclear interests about which all other interests rotate and from which they derive their place and direction. Rational philosophy is also concerned with these things, but the base is broader and the methods are somewhat different, for religion tends not only to focus its concerns, but also to shift the emphasis in attitude and method. There is more of practical urgency in the religious spirit than in the philosophic one. It is harder for it to take the slow, patient path of reasonable scepticism and intellectual discovery, though these often play important if somewhat minor rôles in the drama. Hence it tends to shift from the method of hypothesis to the method of deductive truth, from the speculative to the active mood,

from the relativism of individual difference and judgment
to the universality of authoritative and autonomous doctrine, from the reliance on intellect and sense and taste to
reliance on insight, transport, and the deep compulsion
of moral concern, from reliance on the human mind and
will to reliance on the powers of its discovered truth and
reality.

## II

Such then in theory are the community and divergence
of the ideal of the college and the ideal of religion. Both
are concerned with whatsoever things are good, true, and
beautiful; both seek the release of minds and spirits in
enterprises that make for the highest satisfactions and har-
monies of men, and both rely on all the powers and insights
at our disposal. But the college is the matrix, the alma mater,
of a multitude of offspring, all related by the family bond of
common decency, convention, and understanding, but
each offering to man a somewhat different emphasis and
temperament, a different resolution of the forces running
through his life, a different meaning in the varied proportions of family strains and traditions. Religion perhaps
more than any other member reminds the family of the
ultimate mystery of things and draws them back most constantly to their basic common concerns and deepest
problems.

In the actual practice of recent years, however, the community of interest between liberal learning and high religion

has diminished, and differences have emerged often to the point of mutual mistrust. This gap may have widened because the colleges on the one hand have been getting less liberating, if not less liberal, and religion less 'high" on the other. In any case the churches and the "independent" colleges no longer have the intimacy of either fact or spirit which they once had. The so-called "intellectuals" have drifted away from religious concerns as conventionally understood, and the church for its part has tended to censure and berate the spirit and method of the college.

The blame for this state of affairs lies partly with the church, but no thoughtful person can exonerate the colleges and their faculties. If it is the business of the college to train the mind in the ways of wisdom, and if wisdom is a power to cope with all the basic problems of man's life and destiny, and if religion is, as it seems to have been in human experience, one of the fundamental ways in which man meets many of these problems, then surely the colleges have not fulfilled their obligations and opportunities.

The causes of their negligence are deeply embedded and numerous, but among them are two which have particularly injured the whole liberal enterprise, including the religious one. They are best revealed in the fact that the colleges are not clear about their purpose and are even less articulate in justifying the purposes they do profess. To me the most pathetic fact about the teaching profession is the small proportion among our number, the even smaller proportion among our administrators (let alone the professional "educationalist") who can begin to explain what basically is implied in the "discipline," the "scholarship," and the "citizenship" that constitute their clichés.

Now a mere capacity to define objectives verbally is no assurance that the definition means anything, or that it can serve as a guide for collective action. If it is to do either, the definition must be a living one, a conceptual statement of actual attitudes, insights, sensitivities, and power of full cultivated living. If these are not actually the common property of large proportions of our faculties, no significant definition is possible. It will be form without substance, an imaginary map of an unknown land. Yet the discouraging fact seems to be just this lack of common possession of an inner capacity for full, cultivated living. The accusation may sound excessive and perhaps the demands are excessive, but the fact of the matter is that on most of our campuses far too often the chemist and the poet cannot talk together, nor the physicist and the logician, nor the mathematician and the historian. The economist finds an ethical problem "outside his field," and the artist finds religion a strange superstition. There have been times and there are places where no such state of affairs exists. There is no incurable necessity why it should. But until the situation is cured, we can expect from the colleges relatively empty expressions of purpose with consequently inadequate results.

What, to go deeper, has caused this general paucity of power and insight? Leaving a part of it to the natural and varying limits of the human mind, I should join many of the critics of the day and agree that specialized learning and a misguided use of the "scientific" approach have, by combining forces, accounted for much of it. Why should we expect any other result from our concentrated devotion to specialized learning? If you hold your teacher accountable for a thorough and detailed knowledge of one "field," how can you expect him to devote much attention to neighboring terrain, near or remote? Life is too short—the excessive competitive demand among experts for a knowledge of facts and an operational facility with them as the *sine qua non* of professional competence has, as one might expect, left most other types of intellectual experience and competence to chance. There is much theoretically but little practically to the argument that any field of learning leads ultimately to the understanding of others. My backyard garden is continuous with my neighbor's meadows and the high hills beyond, but I must traverse those meadows and hills to know them and the perspective they can give. Economics, or even chemistry, can lead quickly into ethics or the logic of intellectual method, but rare is the economist or chemist who really explores these related fields, fields that are intrinsically *essential* constituents, rather than neighbors, of the disciplines concerned. The demands of life and the cosmos are legion. How can we as professional exponents of liberal wisdom hope to understand or appreciate them except as we actually and constantly explore the main features, the basic principles of their major areas? This matter of letting only the teacher of government wrestle with political theory and only the logician understand the logic of science has gone too far.

A widespread misguided use of the scientific method and mood has been in league with specialization in its destruction of general cultural sensitivity and power. I am not attacking here a praiseworthy scholarly determination to consider all the relevant factors of a problem and to leave emotional bias and wishful thinking out. Nor am I attacking the specific method of hypothesis and experiment as applied so strikingly to many physical areas of exploration. What I am attacking is an interpretation of "scientific," which ironically and in many areas of exploration tends to fly in the face of undeniable experience or to leave the relevant factors out of account, particularly the essential judgments of value so often necessary to a full understanding of the material at hand. The dramatic success of the "scientific" method in the physical sciences has, in other words, promulgated in the name of "scientific objectivity" a form of wishful thinking in other fields.

The movement of psychology during the twenties toward physiology and behavior and away from philosophy and "inner" experience illustrates the point. Let us take only a part of the logical problem as an example. In physical science, the regular antecedent of an event would have an initial presumption of being a cause of that event and would not be eliminated as such until the event occurred without its presence. In human behavior consciousness, an "inner" idea is usually such an antecedent. The difficulty here is that to date no method has been discovered of eliminating this factor. Simply to disregard it is the rankest wishful thought imaginable. Introspective psychology may have thus far proved fruitless. So far the events it has tried to observe are neither measurable nor open to mutual observation. But for this reason, to deny their existence, or even their relevance, flies in the face of common sense and of intellectual integrity. This is not to assert that something of value may not come from psychology's swing toward physiology and the objective observation of behavior. What I am berating is the illusion that by doing so psychology is treating the problem of *mind* at all, let alone scientifically in any adequate sense of the term. It is an escape, in the name of scientific method, from the perplexities and difficulties of handling that undeniable and essential thing, the mind, which it originally set out to explain and from which it derived its very name and existence as an intellectual pursuit.

"Scientific" psychology is not alone with its illusion; it is merely a peculiarly extreme and doubly ironic illusion because it abandons as unreal the very reality it was originally designed to explain. But many scholars in other areas of study, motivated by "an objective consideration of the facts," have been so preoccupied with this achievement that their capacity to deal with anything except the facts has atrophied. Fearful of being "wishful" interpreters, they have in effect denied that judgments of value about the facts are themselves facts of a higher order; that these facts are also "true" or "false" and that they are an inescapable part of our understanding of man and our achievement of the very wisdom that the study of the facts of experience is supposed to give. We can "statisticize" the economic scene until doomsday, and certainly we ought to know the facts we have to deal with, but this is only a beginning of the problem as to what we ought to do about it, and this is the *essential* thing. To answer this, however, requires, among other things, an appreciable familiarity with what human nature is, what it can be, and what it ought to be. Similarly, the names, dates, attitude, and performance of poets and authors constitute a desirable beginning of knowledge, but the essential problem is the degree of truth and beauty of their works. Why they are good and how we can make their truth a part of us are the great problems, but they are the problems that teachers often hesitate to raise, because they are not "scientifically" approachable questions. One has to believe something to answer them, and this is "wishful thinking." Yet not to answer them is itself a "wishful" answer and a wrong one.

Thus the indifference of the "intellectual" toward religion is really but an inevitable consequence of his lack of general cultural sensitivity. Hence he resists all tendencies to admit value to the scene of intellectual inquiry. Religion, being the most persistent of the agencies thus disposed, is thereby most highly suspect and most vigorously rejected.

These things are matters of balance and discretion, however, and although I feel that intellectualism has pushed its specialization and "objectivity" too far and crowded out concerns that are vital to an adequate understanding of man's deepest and most important problems, and although I think our scholars and administrators are partially culpable for this state of affairs, I cannot admit that their attitude toward religion, as frequently exemplified in its professional and amateur exponents, is wholly unjustified. Neither can I affirm that undergraduate indifference to religion can be explained wholly on the grounds of their philistine upbringing or disposition, or of unfortunate faculty influence. There is often something more basic at work, something that does in fact justify the religious revolt that fires many of our undergraduates.

III

So far as the student is concerned, let us remember what he is in college for. He is there to learn to think for himself and to discover for himself. This proposition is basic to liberal education. The first step in this process is to challenge his assumptions, social, moral, and spiritual, both by critical questioning and by the urging of positive options. As his freshman assumptions stand, whether they be right or wrong, few or many, they are likely to be both simple and blind convictions, acquired from habit and from authority, defensible by him emotionally perhaps, but not rationally. There are a number of risks in this situation. First, simple convictions, even when they have a substantial measure of truth in them, are by virtue of their *simplicity* apt to go wrong. There are no simple formulae for meeting the complexities with which personal and social life present us. "Rugged individualism," "charity for all," "to thine own self be true"—such simple guides, reflecting as they do inarticulate assumptions, when taken uncritically and emotionally, can and indeed often do lead to extravagant personal and social errors, the worse because of the moral halo that appears to justify them. It is only by means of a relatively rich guiding pattern of ideas and values, based on critical understanding, integrated with each other, individually subject to the claims of one another, and collectively modified in their balance and emphasis by the circumstances of life—it is only by such a pattern that we can really hope to meet life adequately.

Secondly, such simple ideas, if they are grounded only in feeling rather than in experience and reason, are apt, when strained by the pressures of the world, either to be discarded completely or to rely on their emotional defenses only and thereby lead to the narrow dogma and bigotry that have caused the world about as much human misery as the "sin" they are aimed to quell. It is, therefore, important that the mind seek rational and experiential justification for its beliefs. Challenge, analysis, explanation, possible alternatives —these and other explorations finally bring the mind to the point where it feels well grounded because it understands why it feels as it does. With this comes a sense of real integrity. They are *my* ideas now, a part of me by virtue of the effort I've devoted to understanding them, by virtue of the reason and experience that I've discovered underlying them, and I accept, reject, modify, integrate them as my intelligence and my conscience dictate.

This is the final hope of the college for each of its students. It is an accomplishment that can usually have but a beginning in college, but it is an attitude, a method, that should endure throughout life, gradually enriching our insights and achievements, and strengthening our convictions.

The rub comes, however (and comes particularly from conventional religious quarters), because of our fear of letting the young mind take such risks. His early years are properly years of indoctrination in the "right" ideas. If these are later "challenged," he is liable to lose the "right" ideas and get the "wrong" ones. I am the last to deny that there is any risk. Given half a chance, a young man will more than occasionally cast off the yoke of his heritage and turn to principles and practices which may bring misery both to himself and to others. But the alternative is also a risk, a greater one, for it can lead to intolerable spiritual poverty and social slavery. Witness the Nazi State. Witness the synagogue of Jesus' time. It was the deadening indoctrination of the Pharisees with their letter-of-the-law and their straining-at-a-gnat that brought on Jesus' revolt. Except as our principles are embedded in understanding there can be no freedom, either personal or social. But the Pharisees we have always with us. They seem to be an inevitable product of institutions, even of the institution of the church. It is these representatives of religion who arouse justifiable suspicion, and unfortunately the prophets among them are too often identified with their company.

In other words, if the colleges must assume some of the blame for spiritual indifference on our campuses, I should maintain with equal vigor that the church or its pastorate and members have also their own shortcomings and are not in a position to cast too many stones. The pomp and ceremony, the moral pretense, the emphasis on petty issues, the heavy reliance on sentiment and on literal authority, the perennial "spiritual gossip," the severity of blame and censorship, these are the things that, as they manifest themselves in the apostles of religion, turn the really sensitive and intelligent person away. Those who do not want to sound their trumpets in the street and to pray at the corners of the synagogue, those who would first cast the beam out of their own eye, those who would not omit the weightier matters of the law, those who would seek the Word and would have it take root in themselves, those who seek not idle words, who would forgive seventy times seven, these are the men of deep religious instinct who find it difficult to identify themselves with the professional apostles and amateur votaries of lesser religious cast.

### IV

Such, then, in summary, are the difficulties of our basic problem of religion and the liberal college. There are differences of emphasis and attitude in religion at its best and liberal education ideally conceived. There are further actual contradictions in practice—the respective professions, the traditions, and human nature being what they are. But we have maintained that in the last analysis the two enterprises have a deep common concern. Both are concerned with the triumph of man, with those truths that will help him to understand his world and see him through his perplexities. The great difference between them is that the one starts man on the quest of discovery, with a map of the total terrain and its numerous promising paths; the other shows him one of the important roads to follow.

The historical fact is that many have found the religious road ineffably rewarding, not merely to the heart, but also to the intellect. The great thinkers who have travelled it are enough to reveal that it cannot be neglected as one of the highways to wisdom. If the liberal college is devoted to the achievement of wisdom, to a study of the best that has been said and done in the world, if it is committed to developing a mind that can cope with all of the enduring problems of mankind, if it professes to deepen and awaken the spirit to its highest achievement, it must perforce, to maintain its integrity and to justify its pretensions, carry the student into *all* the areas of significant human experience, into art and literature, into political and social theory, into science and philosophy, into high religion.

Pretentious it sounds, but there is no other choice if the college is to justify itself. Nor is it a pretension really. Wisdom comes with the years; it is a growth founded on the eternal quest for beauty, goodness, and truth. It is a relative thing, greater in one man than in another and never perfectly achieved. But the college years, the first years of intensive reflection, are those when it is likely to get its greatest conscious impetus—where the ship is launched, the sails are set, and the course is charted.

More specifically, how should the college meet the religious problem? I should say in much the same fashion as it should meet the problem of bringing the student into all the other areas of great achievement. But how does the college do this? The practical difficulties are very real, as the reader will soon observe if he is not already aware of them, but the guiding principles, it seems to me, are clear.

In the first place, the student should concentrate on the best minds of all time. He should read them, understand them as best he can, wrestle with them on the problems they wrestled with; he should study the great books, the great works of art, the masterpieces of music, the great discoveries of religious adventure. Which of them are used is not important so long as they are among the best, sufficiently varied in their point of view, and sufficiently spread over the areas of learning and experience to open up the main channels of basic human concern, achievement, and solution.

In the second place, although a student should have a general notion of the main ideas of a book, his reading should be intensive rather than extensive, with the intensity directed toward the more important ideas the author struggles with. Lincoln was an educated man but he was not an extensive reader. It is reported that the Bible and some plane geometry were the basis of his education. Most of us cannot hope to "cover the ground" that professional scholarship tends to require. But we can struggle to the greatest profit with some of the things that are profound and beautiful in art, literature, politics, science, history, morals, philosophy, and religion.

In the third place, the student should be encouraged by whatever good devices can be found to relate the reading that he does to contemporary events and to his own experience. Conceptual understanding, or "book learning," is, as James, I think, suggests, "the great shorthand of experience," but it is in danger of not being used as such. It can become merely an end in itself, of no help to our practical judgments. Only as we consciously put it to use does it contribute to wisdom. An excellent illustration is the common use of the English Bible. My grandparents never read it "as literature"; they read it as an inspirational experience and as a living guide to conduct and belief. Most laymen who read it usually read it thus, drawing it as they do into the texture of living experience and making of it all at once an esthetic, a moral, and an intellectual thing. It has been left to the colleges to read it as "literature." All literature can thus be falsified, made artificial, the plaything of intellectual amusement. But as we enter into the mind of a great author and he in turn enters into our life, the gap between the mind and the heart, between understanding and action, closes, and we approach a point where knowledge and virtue (or strength) are one. It is at this point that we achieve the basic integration of education, the point at which integration and a kind of integrity become much the same thing because an idea and its fully experienced and appreciated meaning constitute in their fusion an element in the very character of the man.

As a relevant suggestion here, extra-curricular events could, it seems to me, be used with great profit as a device for connecting ideas with student realities—political theory and student government, principles of art and the workshop

and the glee club, ethical theory and fraternity brotherhood, religious study and the college church. The physical
sciences are ahead of us at this point, and the principle is
sound. Ideas get their body from the tissues of direct experience, as they in turn give experience its structure or
form. To isolate them is to enervate their meaning and their
use.

In the fourth place, there is no question that at points the
mind must be taught to deal accurately, intensively, and
thoroughly with facts, and preferably with complexes of
varied types of facts. Most of our living problems are such.
When we face a concrete family or business situation, we
are apt to face a problem with physical, mathematical, economic, psychological, ethical, social, and religious elements.
They must be recognized and dealt with. The principles of
each of these "fields" help to give us our bearings. They
each constitute a kind of compass that points to a principle,
but the actual solution requires a manipulation and resolution of many facts and numerous principles together. Theory and reality merge in a constructive solution or action.

Here we have the basic justification for "integration" as
normally conceived, a kind of transverse integration where
we discover that various "fields" of learning have intrinsic
relationships to one another and to the life and mind of man.
Drawing on them for their facts and insights is another ear-
mark of the educated mind and is a thing which gives wisdom much of its power in life.

Fifth, the student should actively handle his material and
his own ideas, both in speech and in writing. Many a

teacher has said that he learned more in the first year of teaching than in all his previous years put together. Let us take the lesson to heart. He did so because he was held responsible, because he had to do the knowing, the thinking, the lecturing, the writing. Students are no different, and to the extent that they write and think and talk responsibly about the reading they have responsibly done, the keener will be their interest, the deeper their growth and understanding, and the more intense the quest after wisdom.

Behind all this business of content and method, however, lies a possibility that, were it to materialize, would do more to effect the growth of liberal wisdom and religion in our colleges and our students than any other set of devices, for better devices would intrinsically and inevitably follow from it. I have said that specialization and "scientific method" have injured the cause of liberal wisdom and religion by narrowing the range, the general intellectual competence, and the cultural sympathy of our teachers. If these cornerstones of wisdom are to be rebuilt, it can be done only by the wider use of the men who have not lost them and by the wider growth of the men who have. Faculties along with administrators can talk till doomsday about educational theory, but there will be no fiber in the talk unless we are actually willing to do some substantial reading and thinking, and some elementary teaching, so far as is feasible, in one another's "fields."

If this be heresy, then we had better make the most of it. As things now stand, a common purpose living in the hearts and minds of the college community is virtually nonexistent. Few make any pretense of even attempting to understand or appreciate the other man's learning. There is little common cultural core, little foundation on which to build a purpose. Without such purpose, however, the education of the student is left to chance, and the chance is that, like the majority of his teachers, he will take what interests him and neglect the rest, graduating to a life far less wise and far less useful to society than might otherwise be true.

But surely the college can tolerate no such result. Her ultimate reason for existence, her obligations to her heritage and to society compel a higher human purpose and a greater social usefulness. The college has a mission which it must know and preach and practice. Though its nature presupposes within its community a great variety of convictions, often conflicting ones, as to the values of life, there must run through these a common conviction that there is such a thing as a liberal mind, that it can be trained, that if it be liberal it will search eternally for its truths and insights in every great cultural enterprise, be it art, philosophy, science, statesmanship, or religion. Only as most members of the community have some positive intellectual interest and experience in all of these can we emerge from mere negative toleration of one another's fields to a positive mutual understanding and support of their essential features as foundations of liberal wisdom. It then becomes possible to define our purpose, to have it mean something to the total life of the community, and to devise the collaborative means for its achievement.

Talking thus about the liberal program, I may seem to

have wandered from the matter really at stake here—the question of religion in the college. Actually, however, our answer should now be clear, for my thesis has been that like science, like art, like philosophy, like all the great enterprises of the human spirit, religion should be a part, as these are, of the liberal enterprise, and in the same way. The student should by all means explore and struggle with some of the great religious minds and with the basic problems they struggled with. He should certainly have substantial portions of the Bible, something of the best religious thought from Greece, to say nothing of the later great synthesizing poets and expositors such as Dante, St. Thomas, Luther, Calvin, Milton. He should also get a good taste of primitive religious efforts and something of Oriental significance.

The student should study these works in the fashion already suggested, as all such things should be studied. He should study parts of them intensively, and should be encouraged to relate the important ideas in them to his personal and institutional religious life. He should master some of the details of these authors and of the history and influence behind them, and he should write and argue about the ideas at stake.

But once again, for all these books and methods, the college won't really give religion the moral and psychological support it needs until there is a much wider faculty participation in the enterprise. We cannot leave the business solely in the hands of the Department of Religion, the Christian Association, and the College Chapel. The indifference that is currently felt toward all three is contagious and tends, by setting the students' attitude in advance, to destroy for him the very possibility of significant religious achievement. The indifference is deep seated, and the only possible hope for arousing general concern is to devise the means whereby more and more of our faculties will do the requisite reading, thinking, and arguing necessary to credit religion with its due importance in the affairs of civilized men. Such reading and thinking will probably not be done unless it becomes a part of a teacher's vocational responsibility. It can become this if he can participate with others in general courses of more than the usual range. He cannot generally do so with more than elementary courses, but here certainly a liberal scholar ought to accept the challenge, for if there is a common property in these great enterprises he should soon be able to acquire a competence sufficient to guide the struggling neophyte. And as he himself struggles with all this, there is considerable chance, it seems to me, that his own insights and sympathies will grow, and the meaning and value of much that is basic in high religion will capture his interest, respect, and sympathy. The more widely this happens, the greater will be the contagion, and the more likely the student is to find the openings of the religious path and the insights to which they lead.

+·5·+

# The Teaching Office of the Church

THE church is a teacher in more ways than one. It must teach a man the faith; that is, the facts, the principles, the doctrine, the history, which make up a body of content. It must also teach a man how to live in the fellowship of the faithful; that is, the pattern of behaviour and moral conduct which is recognized as Christian character. And it must train a man's spirit so that he has the will to walk the way of faith, to take steps in the dark and to move through the perilous circumstances of life unafraid. An engineering school is expected first and foremost to teach a man how to build a bridge; that is, the theories, techniques, and mechanics of construction. It is not often expected to teach him to walk uprightly on the bridge once it is built, nor is it expected to create in him the will to trust the bridge and to commit himself fearlessly to it. The church must do all three. The scope of its teaching office, therefore, is inclusive of the whole man, his mind, his spirit, and the integration of his mind and spirit with his body, which is character. No fair consideration can be given to the exercise of this office until it is clearly understood how great it is in range and importance.

The difficulties in the way of such an all-inclusive educational program are great at any time, but our own day and age present their own peculiar difficulties of which all Christian teachers should be shrewdly aware. The first is the most universal and serious one: there is no generally accepted framework of faith in the world today. The first Christian teachers, for instance, dealt with men and women who worshipped false gods, half-gods, immoral gods, and sometimes no god at all, but generally speaking there was a framework of divinity within which everyone lived and moved. To be sure, men defied God, were ignorant of God, disobeyed him, misunderstood him, but by and large the word God did not leave a blank on a man's screen of consciousness. It may have stood for no more than the vague feeling that life by and in itself does not explain itself and that there is a mystery at the end of every train of thought which the mind of man cannot completely penetrate. Nevertheless, the word God meant something. In our day, the situation is different. We can take for granted no framework of faith. We are in a time of cultural and religious disintegration. The picture of God has gone. What is more, the frame has gone! In the nineteenth century Christian moral standards were violated more than once, but the fact that men were conscious of violating them, and judged accordingly, is evidence of the fact that they existed. In our day those standards have been not so much violated as forgotten. Obligation, responsibility, duty, self-sacrifice—these words stand for moral ideals which previously have been honored even in the breach of them. Now* they are often without even that poor tribute of honor. In other periods of world history the church could take for granted a framework of faith in which it could place the picture of the faith, whereas now it is not only faith in God revealed in Christ which the church is bound to teach, but it is faith of any kind, in any thing or any person or any God, that the church must stir up in the hearts of the people.

It is not hard to see how this slows up the teaching office of the church. Suppose that a scientific school opened its doors in a country where practically no one believed in the law of cause and effect, very few were convinced of the validity of the experimental method, and only a handful were interested in the pursuit of truth for its own sake! We cannot say that the school would fail but we must admit that its way would be slow and difficult. The contemporary church is in a situation very much like that. It is trying to teach the Christian gospel and the Christian life to a society which instinctively feels that human brawn and brains are enough, that the universe is impersonal, that men are accountable only to themselves, and that when they come to the end of the line they are through and their show is ended. In other words, there is no generally accepted framework of faith, only a tangled network of policies and expedients.

The second difficulty follows closely on the first one's

heels. The church is speaking a language that its people have ceased to speak and only imperfectly understood. The language of the church includes its creeds and ceremonies, its symbolism and sacraments. It is a mighty language and only a fool would presume to discard it and create another to take its place. The church's language about man is in terms of creation, fall, and redemption. The current language that our children learn to speak about man is in terms of evolutionary development, reversion, adjustment, and rehabilitation. True, it is not only a difference of language here, let no one assume that. But the difference of language increases the difficulty of communication. The Ascension of Christ, for instance, represents the centrality of the Christ not only in human life but also in the universe. It is the judgment of the loftiest thinking on the significance of Jesus. But how is the church to communicate that to a generation that speaks the language of interstellar spaces and astronomical immensities? To be sure it can be done, but not without considerable difficulty. Imagine again a scientific school trying to teach students for whom the words gravity, induction, law, causation, have been practically emptied of their meaning. It could be done, but only by those who appreciated the discrepancy in language. No, the difficulty of language is by no means an insuperable one, but it may become so if the man who is speaking is unaware of the fact that the man he is speaking to does not understand a word he says.

Added to these difficulties is the fact that the majority of people are continually exposed to impressions that are anything but Christian. The most powerful creators of current impressions are the movies, the radio, the newspapers, and the public schools. The movies invariably leave the impression that virtue is dull, crime exciting, and immorality accredited. The radio leaves the impression that advertising, not honesty, counts and that the public is to be exploited to the maximum of its gullibility. The newspapers contribute their share to the same impression in that their policies are often dictated by the interests of their largest advertisers and by the lowest common denominator of the human thirst for scandal. The public schools, by and large, leave the impression that religion plays no essential part in the life of educated men, that the church takes second or third place, and that the enlightened man or woman has graduated from both. There are, of course, exceptions in every case. There are brave Christian editors, and Christian teachers and principals who successfully infuse into their work the spirit of Christianity. There are Christians in the radio world and even in the movie industry a devout man might be found here and there. All praise and thanks to their leavening influence! But they must not blind us to the fact that the teachers of the Christian church are facing competitors who hold the key positions in the contemporary strategy, that they have at their disposal the best modern technique, unlimited financial reserves, and that they operate twenty-four hours a day, seven days a week.

II

Granted the almost insuperable difficulties that Christian teachers face, what shall be their first step? To my mind, there is only one answer: Let them clarify their own minds. No teacher can teach anything unless the thing he is trying to teach is as clear as day to himself. Can the church pass that test? It does not generally appear so. More and more it becomes apparent that the teaching of the church lacks power because its teachers lack confidence, and that they lack confidence because they are confused in their own minds. Generally speaking, their wills are not confused. Be it said to the everlasting honor of the leaders of the Christian church, great and small, that however confused they may be in their minds, they stand unashamedly for Christ and the way of life that is consistent with him. They may be ineffective, but not insincere.

The reason for this intellectual confusion is not hard to find. In the last hundred years or so more new facts have been fed the human mind than in the last two thousand years. It is not surprising that the religious mind finds it difficult to digest them. Copernicus was finally digested by the church, but hardly had that feat of assimilation been performed when along came Darwin, Huxley, Jeans, Harnack, Einstein, and Freud! They were a dose too big to digest over night. There are some Christians who blithely ignore these men and the facts that they unearthed but Christians for the most part have never tried to divorce themselves from the actual world in which they lived.

Their religion is a religion of fact and consequently they reverence facts wherever they find them. The church, therefore, cannot be true to itself, nor can it be a successful teacher, until it has assimilated all the facts that have been uncovered, sifted them, evaluated them, and rewritten its own teaching in the light of them. This is by no means to make the church subservient to every passing intellectual fad, nor does it imply any disloyalty to its own peculiar understanding of the truth. It does make the church the servant, and interpreter, of fact, in the light of the Supreme Fact whose minister and agent she is.

To be specific, in a universe which has been impersonalized by science, exactly what does the church mean by a personal God? Personal in what sense? And how shall people picture such a God? What shall they expect of him? The benevolent figure has faded from the sky and so far the church has put nothing in its place. When we pray, to whom shall we pray and what have we the right to expect of him? When the church talks about the providence of God, exactly what does it mean and how shall it be made real to people brought up on the diet of cause and effect? Or, how does the church understand the miraculous elements in her own Scriptures? How shall it be made relevant to a world which has long since ceased to think in terms of miracles? How shall the real content and value of the miracle stories be carried over into a world that is impatient with the antiquated vehicle? Again, precisely what does the church mean by the fall of man and how does the story of Adam and Eve relate to our current sense of guilt and remorse? Does the church believe that man was once perfect or does it not? What does the church mean by sin and how shall it be interpreted in such a way as to influence the moral conduct of people brought up under the impression that they are accountable to no one but themselves? Just what does the church mean by love and how shall it be applied to a world situation which seems to exclude the love-ethic as even a remote possibility? What does the church mean by the atonement and how is the cross to be the saving power in human life? What is the authority of the church's teaching—the dictated word of God, the infallible voice of the chief bishop, or the inspired word of God spoken by dedicated, though fallible, men?

This list of questions could be prolonged interminably, but the list is already long enough to indicate that the teachers of the church must do some hard thinking and some effective recreating if they are to make any progress in the education of an un-churched generation in the way of Christian belief and practice. For it is not only the people who are confused; that would be a relatively simple matter. But there is also evidence of confusion in the minds of the leaders themselves, a confusion understandable but not to be tolerated indefinitely.

It should be clearly understood that we neither want nor expect the kind of clarity that is the product of over-simplification, nor do we want the clarity which is bought at the expense of the fundamental integrity of Christian truth. But we must have that clarity which is the result of straight thinking and profound feeling united in a single effort to bring the eternal truth of God to bear upon the fretful lives of the sons of time.

No single person can hope to clarify the mind of the church. It must be accomplished by a union of the best minds applied to the toughest problems of faith and life. It took three hundred years or more to clarify the mind of the church in terms of ancient and classical thought. We need not be surprised if it takes at least that long to do it again in the terms of the mysterious universe which has been described to us by the modern pioneers of thought. There will be local clearings, here and there, the fruit of individual minds pressing further and further toward the frontiers of truth. Mistakes will be made, but there will be advances, which will in time be consolidated in a united Christian mind.

No Christian teacher, however, can afford to wait for the outcome of a modern Nicaea. He must begin now. In spite of the difficulties imposed from without and the confusion within, there never was a greater urgency forcing the hand of the Christian teacher. Those whose lives have been wrecked by the war must be taught how to salvage them, how to accept losses and disappointments, how to use the Christian resources of recuperative power, how to make life under entirely new conditions. Those who are coming along, as yet unscathed by war, must be taught the principles of Christian thought and practice which they, in turn, must incorporate into the political and economic structures which are now in the process of creation. Never was there greater need for the church to make it unmistakably plain just where it stands on every major issue of life.

### III

With a mind as clear as possible, and fully aware of the serious difficulties in its way, the Christian church sets about its teaching ministry. There are at least five channels through which Christian teaching normally proceeds. The first is the church school.

The school is concerned primarily with content, with the presentation of facts. The church school, therefore, is the logical place to instruct young Christians, to teach them the doctrine of the church, its history, its Bible, its habits and customs, its way of worship, and its moral principles. Too often the fruits of Christian living have been expected of those who have no roots in the fundamentals which are the soil in which the plant grows. The urbanity and wisdom of a Justice Holmes are grounded in a technical knowledge of law and jurisprudence and to look for the first without the second would be pure folly. Likewise, the loving spirit of a Christian saint is grounded in the fundamentals of Christian belief and principle.

Given so great a task, it is all the more tragic that the church schools have been so generally inadequate. The Sunday school is the butt of criticism of pupils, parents, teachers, and clergy. There are, of course, rare and distinguished exceptions, but generally speaking, the Protestant Sunday school has been a failure. Pupils resist it even more than they do day-school, teachers shirk its responsibilities and disciplines, parents have little confidence in it, and the clergy are well aware of its inadequacy. In nine cases out of ten the equipment is poor, the teaching second-rate, the time insufficient, and the results negligible.

The first step toward a remedy is for the Christian churches to ask themselves the question: Is Christian education important? If it is not, it would be far better to drop it altogether than to continue it in the halfhearted way that has prevailed during the last century. If it is, let us expend upon it the same amount of time and money and interest that we lavish upon secular education. In some cases that will mean parochial schools owned and operated by the church. On the whole such a policy is not in accord with our principle of public education. Whether or not the weekday religious education of children released from the public school for a certain period each week will solve our problem it is too early in the experiment to say. One thing that is to be desired is that the principles of religion and ethics be given some place in the curriculum of *every* school. There would be the broad base of religious assumptions upon which the churches might build their own superstructure of doctrine and worship. If Christian truth is truth about the universe, penetrating every atom of its life and permeating even its most secular aspect with meaning and purpose, then it is hard to see how religious and secular education can be permanently divorced. We have tried that in this country for the last fifty years or more and it has given us generations of men and women completely ignorant of the moral and spiritual backgrounds of our civilization and culture. The Christian church neither desires nor intends to control public education. Two schools, one public and the other parochial, are a contradiction of the very essence of the universality of Christian truth. A step toward a solution would be the inclusion of primary religious education in the public schools and improved advanced religious education in the church schools.

The second channel is the small group. Given a generation who know practically nothing about the Christian framework and consequently find themselves helpless to practice the Christian virtues when they are most desperately needed, what can the church do? It can gather together small groups of men and women, united by a common desire and interest, and instruct them in the basic facts of Christianity. That is what Isaiah did. Jesus did it. It is the cultivation of the small group that promises the greatest fruit. Obviously, interest will not be confined to the facts and figures of religion, but will include the more subtle and delicate matters involved in the training and disciplining of the spirit. Groups for young married couples, groups for college students, for working men and women, for advanced students of the spiritual life—these groups are waiting to be fed. A young man or woman may set religion aside during his student days, but when he becomes a parent, he is forced to think of the spiritual welfare of his child. What will he teach him? What will he say when he asks: Where is God? At that moment the young parent is ready to be taught. Business men and women will be approachable from other angles. They will be concerned with the issues which involve the whole world as well as themselves, and they will be searching for the clear light of Christian truth in regard to these issues. In small groups the shy person can be encouraged to speak his mind and the precocious talker can be quite easily restrained. The leader of the group is not only making official pronouncements, he is also listening to questions, balancing objections, clarifying misconceptions, wiping away prejudices, illuminating dark and treacherous avenues of thought. No privilege is greater than the privilege that comes to a Christian minister as he sits down with a carefully selected group of interested men and women and carefully leads them through the paths of truth. If the world is to be saved for Christianity and if the Christian church is to be the agent of its salvation, the chances are that the work will be performed not by mass meetings or thronged churches, but by small groups of eager, yet humble people who care so much that they are willing to listen, to think, to rethink, to work, and to sacrifice.

The third channel is the sermon. The sermon is as much a part of worship as the waves are a part of the sea. Worship is the exposure of a man's whole being to the reality of God and the exertion of all his energies thitherwards. If worship is to be thought of in terms of *ex*posure, the sermon might well be thought of in terms of *dis*closure. Every Christian sermon has as its primary aim the revelation of some aspect of the reality of God as he is known to us in Christ. A sermon is not a lecture, nor a discourse, a homily, or instruction. Its primary object is not to present objective information, and therefore the sermon was not put in the first place among the available channels of Christian teaching. It assumes the content that the school has already given to the pupil. Yet, the sermon can be a strong arm of the church's teaching office. There are some sermons, for instance, which are more didactic than others. Sermons on the great Christian doctrines of God, of Christ, of man, and of redemption will involve a sound factual basis. The unique function of the sermon, however, is not so much to instruct. It is to reveal, to draw the curtains aside from the great realities of life, to stir the hidden and hitherto untouched moral and spiritual energies of a man, to unveil, to disclose, to make known the nature of things, and more especially the nature of God as we behold him in the character of Jesus Christ. The sermon, therefore, is more peculiarly adapted to the training of a man's spirit, so long as it is clearly understood that there is no real division between a man's mind and spirit. It is a matter of accent. The preacher should not forget the teaching possibilities of a sermon. The whole attitude involved in the modern criticism of the Bible can be created (not catapulted, be it noted) in the minds and spirits of a congregation by the continual reference by the preacher to principles and practices of historical criticism as they are illustrated by the text of the sermon. The kingdom of God is not going to come by way of instruction, but sermons on the parables can hardly fail to throw light on the nature of the kingdom, without which light men will find it difficult to prepare themselves for it. The preaching of the first Christians was not intended to instruct their listeners but rather to tell them the momentous news that God had raised up Jesus whom they slew and hanged on a tree. Yet, in the very telling there were the seeds of truth, and even in those days of extreme urgency, the Christian evangelists were at the same time teachers and doctors.

## IV

There are still two other channels through which Christian teaching may flow, the liturgy and the personal consultation. In liturgical churches movement, color, light, word, are united in a pattern of dramatic action. You can teach a child the principles of reverence from now until doomsday with slight possibility of success. Bring him into a church in which the movement of the people is reverent, proceeding along well-worn paths of traditional behaviour, and he may become reverent by participating in its practice. Teach a child about the holiness of the Almighty God and your efforts may all be in vain until you have brought him into the temple where sincere men and women bow down before the Holy One. A man can lecture night and day upon the meaning of the Last Supper and yet find his class completely devoid of anything but an academic knowledge of it. Bring them to a church where the faithful have met together to take part in that great meal. Let him see the bread broken, and the wine poured out; let him hear the words solemnly repeated, "This is my body which is given for you"; and let him watch the faithful go toward the altar, kneel as a sign of their dependence and their devotion, lift empty hands which in turn are filled with the Bread of Life; let him see them come away as though refreshed in body and spirit, and rededicated to him to whom their whole lives shall be an offering. He may not believe the theories about the sacrament; he may not be convinced of its intellectual validity, but he has seen it in action and is a witness to its reality. No one can witness a communion service according to any rite or liturgy and not know that Christianity is breaking, giving, feeding, loving, serving, receiving. It tells the things of heaven yet it surrounds the most commonplace things of life with all the glory and reverence of which man is capable. Bread and wine—the simplest things, yet they are vehicles of the most sublime of which the mind of man dares dream. More than all the lectures on sacramental theology, such participation in the liturgy of the church can teach the hearts of the faithful. Not one without the other, of course; but both.

Finally, there is presented the most sacred of all opportunities when a Christian minister and a single individual sit down to consider that person's life with its peculiar problems and possibilities. It is the opportunity of the personal consultation. The Protestant church has rejected the Catholic confessional and doubtless there are many abuses of that discipline which should be corrected. The Protestant church, on the whole, eliminated not only the abuses but also the rich opportunities which the confessional provided and in most cases it has created nothing to take its place. Speaking in general terms, the Protestant church has forfeited completely the direction of its people's personal life. Sermons, no matter how powerful, are of necessity general. It is easy for a man to slip through them without ever applying them to the specific instance of his own moral and spiritual need. The training of the spirit of a man cannot be done entirely and completely in public. It must be done in privacy, yet not altogether in solitude. The sinner needs the spiritual director, the discouraged man needs the sympathetic ear, the misguided man needs the skilled counselor. Some people will find their way to the minister even when no encouragement is offered. But most people will find their way to those who are poorly qualified to handle the delicate situation presented by their hopes and fears. No matter what a man believes about sacramental absolution, he cannot appropriate the forgiveness of God by himself. It must be administered, as a judge administers justice and a physician administers health. Special opportunity, therefore, should be provided for timid and untrained men and women. Let it be known that the minister is free at certain stated intervals to do nothing but meet with individuals who are looking for guidance. It cannot be gotten out of a book; it cannot be entirely derived from listening to a sermon or a lecture. It works man to man. It presents the unlimited opportunity of leading men along the way of Christian truth as it applies to the places where they really live. Without such opportunities the whole teaching office of the church is in danger of being bloodless and unrelated to the actual lives of men and women. A man may know the Bible by heart, the creeds and commandments backwards and forwards, the Prayer Book better than his own name, and still not be able, by himself, to make the contact with the waters of life without which his spirit will die of thirst. The personal consultation, therefore, is the crown of the school, the sermon, the group, and the liturgy.